Appledore Quay fifty years ago. Tom Schiller is the tall lad in the group, Rees Scilly next to him. The *Rosamund Jane* was one of the last of the coasting smacks. Three gravel barges are drying their sails and there is a forest of masts upstream. *National Maritime Museum*

OUT OF APPLEDORE

PUBLICATIONS BY BASIL GREENHILL

The Merchant Schooners (2 volumes)
Sailing for a Living
Out of Appledore (with W J Slade)
Boats and Boatmen of Pakistan
Steam and Sail (with Rear Admiral P W Brock)
Westcountry Coasting Ketches (with W J Slade)
A Victorian Maritime Album
The Coastal Trade (with Lionel Willis)
A Quayside Camera
Archaeology of the Boat
Edited and Prefaced: The Last Tall Ships, by Georg Kåhre
The Life and Death of the Sailing Ship
Schooners
The British Seafarer Discovered (with Michael Mason)

BY BASIL GREENHILL AND ANN GIFFARD

Westcountrymen in Prince Edward's Isle
The Merchant Sailing Ship: A Photographic History
Travelling by Sea in the Nineteenth Century
Women Under Sail
Victorian & Edwardian Sailing Ships
Victorian & Edwardian Ships and Harbours
Victorian & Edwardian Merchant Steamships

OUT OF
APPLEDORE

*The autobiography of a coasting shipmaster and
shipowner in the last days of wooden sailing ships*

by

W. J. SLADE

Master Mariner

Edited and with a new Preface by
Basil Greenhill,
Director, The National Maritime Museum

CONWAY MARITIME PRESS

© Conway Maritime Press Ltd
2 Nelson Road, Greenwich, London SE10 9JB

First Published   1959
Revised Edition 1972
Third Edition   1974
Fourth Edition   1980

ISBN 0 85177 026 6

Dedicated by Author and Editor to the memory of
Gillian Greenhill

Printed in Great Britain by
R J Acford, Chichester

CONTENTS

EDITORIAL PREFACE   ix

CHAPTER 1   How It All Began   1
CHAPTER 2   I Become Master   23
CHAPTER 3   The First World War   39
CHAPTER 4   The Coming of the Motors   54
CHAPTER 5   The Depression and an Interlude in Sail
             Again   74
CHAPTER 6   The Second World War and the End of It All   96

APPENDIX 1   List of the Vessels Owned by the Slade Family
              of Appledore 1888-1948 compiled by H.
              Oliver Hill   107
APPENDIX 2   Notes on the Racing of Schooners and Ketches
              by W. J. Slade   117
APPENDIX 3   Note by Captain J. Whitefield, D.S.C.,
              corroborating W. J. Slade's narrative   ...   123

ILLUSTRATIONS

Frontispiece

Appledore Quay fifty years ago. Tom Schiller is the tall lad in the group, Rees Scilly next to him. The *Rosamund Jane* was one of the last of the coasting smacks. Three gravel barges are drying their sails and there is a forest of masts upstream.

Plate 1   *Facing page* 10

The ketch *Alpha*, built near Truro in Cornwall, which was purchased by the Slade family in 1897.

Plate 2   *Facing page* 11

W. J. Slade's father, William Kingdon Slade, at about the time of his marriage.

Plate 3   *Facing page* 11

W. J. Slade's mother, Rosina Annie Abigail Harding, from a photograph taken at the same time as that of her husband in Plate 2.

Plate 4   *Facing page* 11

Although positive identification is impossible, after fifty years, it seems almost certain that these three small boys on the hard below Appledore Quay are the cousins, W. J. Slade (left), Thomas Slade (centre) and Richard Slade (right) working on one of the grandfather's boats. All became successful shipmasters and owners.

Plate 5   *Facing page* 26

The Boys of Appledore half a century ago, a group of W. J. Slade's youthful contemporaries, later to become the last generation of British coasting sailing ship masters and owners. They are, left to right:– Powe, Mike Powe, S. Peake, W. Blackmore (who was near his home, so he still had his boots and stockings on), J. Hammett, E. Yeo and J. H. Peake.

Plate 6   *Facing page* 26

A painting by George Quance of the ketch *Alpha*.

Plate 7   *Facing page* 27

Appledore boys could scull a boat like men at an early age. In the background are gravel barges waiting for the tide.

Plate 8   *Facing page* 27

The ketch *Maud Mary*, owned for many years by the Slades, the ketch *Thomas* coming up the Torridge under mainsail, and the small ketch *Trio* (not the Slade's *Trio* but another Appledore vessel) outward bound from Appledore.

Plate 9   *Facing page* 42

The topsail schooner *Doris* built at Salcombe and owned by the Slade family from 1910 until her loss on the French coast in 1918.

Plate 10   *Facing page* 43

At Appledore boys and girls became intimately familiar with boats as soon as they could walk.

Plate 11   *Facing page* 58

The ketch *Trio* of which W. J. Slade was master at the end of the first world war.

Plate 12   *Facing page* 58

The old Quay from the west. The 'sailing barge alongside was called the *Mirre*. The hulk was the brigantine *Oak*.

Plate 13   *Facing page* 59

The ketch *Margaret*, owned by Jack Lamey, a sailmaker, outward bound down the channel from Appledore to the bar. The man standing on the beach is Thomas Powe, who earned a living as a winchman discharging vessels.

Plate 14   *Facing page* 59

John Cann, Samuel Berry and John Cawsey, gravel bargemen, yarning on the Quay. The bows of the ketch *Emu* and the stern of the ketch *Advance* are also in the picture.

Plate 15   *Facing page* 74

A ketch off the end of the Quay, towards the top of the tide, salmon boats in the foreground.

Plate 16   *Facing page* 74

The *Millom Castle* as a " set of jugs."

Plate 17   *Facing page* 75

The *Haldon* when she was first rigged to W. J. Slade's design as a three-masted schooner.

Plate 18   *Facing page* 75

A dozen vessels and several gravel barges lying side by side off Appledore Quay.

Plate 19   *Facing page* 90

W. J. Slade's father, his brother George, and an uncle, on board the *M. A. James* after she was brought home to Appledore. William Kingdon Slade was 65 years old when this photograph was taken.

Plate 20   *Facing page* 91

There was always a crowd at the slip where the ferry from Instow landed. The man with the bowler hat is probably " Daddy " Johns, one of the ferrymen.

INTRODUCTION TO THE SECOND EDITION

This book is the life story of a British coasting seaman, shipmaster, and shipowner, in the last years of small wooden merchant sailing ships, written by himself. It is a unique record, a first hand account of a very old way of life which has now completely vanished, and which is very much a part of the history of Britain. The record is the more valuable because it covers the period when that way of life made a partly successful attempt to adapt itself to the changes that were going on around it, before it was finally lost in the general development of the modern world.

It falls to very few men to be almost the sole means of preservation of any record of the way of life they followed. This has been W. J. Slade's particular privilege. Through this book and through his very significant contribution to the writing of *The Merchant Schooners* he has saved the last years of one of the oldest industries from oblivion. There is, as far as I know, only one other comparable record, Captain Hugh Shaw's autobiography which he has deposited in the manuscript collection of the National Maritime Museum.

I have, with Mr. Slade's help, written at length in the two volumes of *The Merchant Schooners* about the historical background which gave rise to the way of life which Mr. Slade followed. Until the development of the internal combustion engine and modern industrial centralisation almost every small port around the coast of Britain, and particularly of Western England and Wales, had its own fleet of small wooden merchant sailing ships, at first brigs, brigantines, and small single-masted vessels, sloop or cutter rigged, and usually described as cargo smacks, and later, in large numbers in the second half of the nineteenth century and the first twenty years of this, schooners with two or three masts, and ketches.

Many of these ships were deep water traders, carrying many cargoes all over the world. But towards the end of the last century, as the scale of industry and the size of cargoes offering increased, these small deep water sailing vessels tended to become specialised in certain trades. The greatest of these was the trade between Europe and the North and South Americas and the West Indies, a trading pattern which had as its backbone the carrying of salted codfish from Newfoundland and Labrador for European markets. This trade, and with it the small deep water sailing ships, died out after the first world war with the rising standard of living in Western Europe and the ready availability of other and more appetising forms of cheap nutritious food. The surviving small British sailing ships went into the coastal trade, where they persisted in considerable numbers until the second world war, and even, a few of them, afterwards. Thus the small wooden schooner and ketch were frequently to be seen long after the big commercial square rigged sailing ship had become a curiosity. They persisted as a kind of eighteenth century relic into the second half of the twentieth century.

The hard deep water trades set the standard for the small sailing ships, the great bulk of which were employed from time to time, and many all the time, in the home trade about the British Isles and in near Continental waters. Some ports were predominantly deep sea ports with purely coasting vessels as well as their Atlantic Schooners, like Portmadoc in North Wales and Fowey in Cornwall. Some were chiefly home trade ports with a certain number of vessels sometimes or often taken up for ocean voyages. Such were the ports of the Lancashire coast, Bridgwater in Somerset and Appledore, with its sister towns and villages of Braunton, Bideford and Barnstaple, in North Devon.

Appledore had a tremendous reputation for its ships and seamen and in the latter part of the nineteenth century the large scale of its ship owning enterprise, in relation to the size of its population, was remarkable. Moreover, because of its geographical position, its shipowning and seafaring traditions, and the business acumen of the owners, shown especially in their adoption of the auxiliary diesel engine early in this century, Appledore survived with its sister village of Braunton, across the estuary, as a sailing ship port long after sails had died out altogether (and with them usually the small ports themselves) elsewhere in Britain. The North Devon rivers, the Torridge and the Taw, were the last homes of cargo carrying sailing ships with all their attendant services and skills in these islands. And these ships were small wooden sailing vessels near to the types of ship upon which man's conquest of the oceans was founded. The last of them, the ketch *Irene*, and the schooner *Kathleen & May*, did not cease sailing until 1960.

William James Slade was born at Appledore on April 28, 1892, the eldest son of William Kingdon Slade of Appledore, himself the son of a deep water sailor and employed at the time of his son's birth as the master of a local ketch rigged coasting sailing vessel, the *Francis Beddoe*. W. J. Slade's mother was Rosina Annie Abigail Harding Slade, the daughter of an Appledore ship-master and an experienced sailor in her own right in those days when it was the local custom for the girls and women of Appledore often to be at sea with their men.

At the time W. J. Slade was born, his family, the male members of which had previously been employed as seamen in the deep water square rigged vessels which used to sail from Appledore in the North American trade and as mates and masters in the home trade, were just beginning to establish them-selves as independent coasting shipowners. The initial capital was accumulated through the efforts of one of his father's sisters. With what she saved she was able to buy outright for her husband, George Quance, a former seaman in clipper ships and an artist and raconteur of some local reputation, a small ketch of his own, the *Nouvelle Marie*. This was in the year 1888. In 1895 William Kingdon Slade and his mother bought the ketch *Heather Bell*, already 25 years old. The family so prospered that in the next four years they were able to buy two outstanding vessels, the *Alpha* and the *Ulelia*, both built by Charles Dyer at Sunny Corner near Truro as fore and aft schooners for the North Atlantic trade. These two ships were re-rigged by the Slades as ketches, their new mast and sail plans were drawn out by George Quance, and they proved themselves fast, economical, and profitable vessels in the coasting trade. In the course of the next thirty years no less than eighteen ships were purchased by the Slade family. Notes on each of these ships are given in the first appendix to this book, which H. Oliver Hill has prepared. By the outbreak of the second world war the Slade family, with four three-masted schooners and a ketch, had become the last considerable owners of merchant auxiliary sailing ships in Britain. The chartering of the majority of their ships by the Govern-ment for defence purposes during the war brought this ship-owning story to an end and the Slades of the present generation have distinguished themselves in other professions.

W. J. Slade was taken to sea by his mother at the age of a few months in the *Francis Beddoe*, and henceforth he was at sea for a month every year. His earliest recollections are of the lovely *Alpha*, of which his father became master and part owner in 1897, when he was five years old. At the age of twelve he left school to become boy under his father in her sister ship, the *Ulelia*. As his father was only partly literate he was compelled not only to work as a member of the crew but also to do much of the ship's business under his father's direction.

A highly intelligent and sensitive boy W. J. Slade rapidly learned the intricacies of a coasting shipowner's and shipmaster's business and this early training helped greatly towards his own later prosperity in this branch of shipping. But, dogged by seasickness throughout his seagoing career, he was never really reconciled to the discomforts and crudities of the life in small merchant schooners and ketches, with their rudimentary accommodation, their inadequate protection against wind and weather, the poor food of the days before the auxiliary engine, and the backbreaking labour of working their heavy gear. In due course through hard training under his exacting father he became a highly skilful and successful master and owner of sailing and auxiliary vessels, delighting in the more testing problems of practical sailing ship seamanship and coastal navigation. He prospered through the difficult change from pure sail to auxiliary motor power. But he was always as much aware of the limitations of his way of life as he was of its merits, which are, perhaps, nowadays sometimes somewhat oversung, and this awareness enriches his narrative.

At the age of seventeen young Slade became mate of the schooner *Elizabeth Jane* under his father, and two years later he was put in charge of her as master. At twenty-three he owned one quarter of the schooner *Millom Castle;* he married and bought his own house. At twenty-five he was master and part owner of the schooner *W.D.Potts* and he subsequently commanded the ketch *Trio*, the *Millom Castle* in which he had his most serious fight with a gale, and the schooner *M.A.James.* The vessel with which he was longest associated and in which he made most of his fortune was the ketch, later a three-masted schooner, *Haldon.* He sold her and retired in 1943. Although in some ways the least satisfactory of them all, the *Haldon* was the only one of the Slade ships still afloat and in commission when Mr. Slade wrote his autobiography. She had been rebuilt as a fully powered motorship and was trading in Iceland waters in the late nineteen fifties.

Giving as it does details not only of seamanship and ship management, ownership and navigation, but also of the financial and social background of these ships, Mr. Slade's narrative is a fascinating and most valuable record. This is a part of the history of the sailing ship and at the same time part of the story of the village life of England. It is industrial and social history at first hand. Mr. Slade's narrative links us with a world we have completely lost.

The vessels of which Mr. Slade writes were lovely to look at. Their sails, patched grey and brown, were set above hulls usually black. Many of them, particularly those which had been built for the deep water trades, were of beautiful hull form. The schooners, with their yards and square topsails and great mainbooms, seemed descended straight from the great days of sailing ships. The smell of the tarred rigging, the tall solid wooden masts, so thick where they grew from the decks, the polished wheel or great carved and decorated tiller out in the open with no protection against the weather for the helmsman, the heavy ropes and huge hand operated windlass in the bows, the master's cabin right in the stern of the ship with its polished panels and shaped scrubbed table, the dark forecastle with its characteristic fusty smell, all seemed in the later days of the coastal sailing ships like survivals from another century; which, indeed, is exactly what they were.

They were the last commercial links with the ancient skills of mast and sail, when each voyage was an adventure in greater or lesser degree, when the small capital necessary for seafaring enterprise could be raised within the village community, if not within the circle of the family itself. W. J. Slade tells of a life in which every man, woman and child was dependent on the fortunes of those who pitched their skill against wind and weather in small wooden vessels. It was a simple, rough, and hard life, and too often it was a poverty stricken life. Although it really ended only thirty years ago, it was perhaps in many ways more akin to the life of the eighteenth century than of the twentieth. It bred its characters, the dominant father from whose moral power the sons and daughters escaped, or did not escape, only after a long struggle as much with themselves as with him. And those remarkable seafaring women, skimping and saving in the background, sharing to a large extent in the work of the men, guiding and ruling and keeping a sense of humour through generations of toil and hardship.

Mr. Slade sometimes says that Appledore at the time when he first went to sea was a hundred years behind the times. Little has so far been written of its early history. The study is a difficult one because for centuries the village was within the parish of Northam, a settlement a mile or two up the hill, and it has never been a port in the official sense, that is, the headquarters of an area administered by a Collector of Customs. At various times in its history it has been a part of the Port of Barnstaple and at others a part of the Port of Bideford, as it is today and was throughout Mr. Slade's sea career. Most of the time as a shipbuilding and outfitting place, a source of seamen and shipmasters, it has served both ports.

For a thousand years there must have been a settlement of mariners, fishermen, boatbuilders and shipowners at this obvious point of confluence of the Taw and the Torridge where the sheltering hill protects the strand against the Atlantic gales. Its development, as might be expected, seems to have taken place in fits and starts. Westcote, writing "A View of Devonshire in 1630", records a burst of activity in late Elizabethan and Stuart times, for he speaks of it as having expanded within living memory from a poor settlement to a place which, "now for fair buildings and multiplicity of inhabitants and houses, it doth equal divers market towns, and is furnished with many good and skilful mariners."

Presumably he was referring to what for many years was called East Appledore, the area immediately north and west of the present Richmond

Drydock. Here a settlement grew up around a triangular sheltered bay, the best place for small vessels to lie in the whole river. Part of one of the grand buildings of this little settlement, now known as Docton House, is still standing. It was probably there when North Devon ships with Appledore men in their crews set out from the Torridge in 1586 to make the second attempt from Britain at permanent settlement in the North American Continent.

The cod fishery of the shallow seas off Newfoundland and Nova Scotia, in Massachusetts Bay and in the Gulf of St. Lawrence, drew Europeans from the end of the fifteenth century. The misty often stormy waters were the first of the successive frontiers which have played such a fundamental part in North America's history. Salt fish was an important item in European diet because it has certain qualities which make it very valuable in a technically primitive society – it is easily preserved for long periods and it retains its food value. It makes easily transportable provender for armies on the march and merchant ships on long voyages. It remained a staple diet in Europe until fifty years ago, and it still is much eaten in the West Indies and in West Africa. In developed societies it has now become something of a luxury, but every supermarket in eastern North America stocks Nova Scotia salt cod.

Despite pioneering efforts from Bristol in the fifteenth century British merchants were slow to exploit the North American fishery. But by 1625 Barnstaple, including Appledore, was sending ships to the fishery by the score, and it was probably the development of the Newfoundland trade which gave rise to the expansion of Appledore to which Westcote referred. During the seventeenth century, partly because of the silting up of the River Taw on which it stands, Barnstaple gave pride of place as a port to Bideford. In 1700 thirty Bideford ships sailed from Newfoundland, thirteen of them for Portugal and the Mediterranean, as against twelve ships from Barnstaple and sixteen from Dartmouth. Only London, with forty-five ships, had more vessels than Bideford in the Newfoundland fishery.

Because North Devon was so deeply involved in the North Atlantic fishing it was natural that the nearly empty outward bound fishing ships should carry people from the coastal areas, people who were already familiar with the idea of an Atlantic crossing and had some hearsay knowledge of what lay beyond. Thus men and women from Appledore became New Englanders in colonial times. As early as 1620 seven ships, some of Barnstaple and some of Bideford, sailed from the latter port for North America. The products of the local potteries formed a valuable part of the trade. In recent years fragments of identifiable North Devon pottery have been excavated from Colonial sites all down the eastern seaboard from Massachusetts to Virginia. An extensive carrying trade in tobacco developed. According to some sources by 1720 Bideford had outdistanced all the other ports of south-west Britain except

Bristol in the amount of tobacco it imported, though the port handled only a small fraction of London's turnover. Great quantities of Irish wool came into the River Torridge to feed the large cottage textile industry in North Devon.

Architectural evidence shows the effects of this eighteenth century activity when something of the general flavour of modern Appledore must have been established. It is in parts a village of groups of Georgian cottages, some with large first-floor windows which may once have illuminated sail or mould lofts, joined together with houses of later construction.

At this period Thomas Benson, a prominent merchant in the North American trade, built a new quay down the west side of East Appledore's sheltered triangular bay. On this quay shipbuilding developed and small houses were built up the hillside behind it. The hamlet of Irsha, West-Appledore, a poor place away on the northern headland, began to grow also.

But during the later eighteenth century the great North American trade Bideford had built up in the preceding hundred years gradually died away from the effects of the long wars with their attendant high insurance and manning costs and because, perhaps, of the conservatism of some of the local merchants who persisted in outdated trading practices in the Newfoundland business, and because high duties on tobacco brought the investment required for the business beyond local resources. The town's overseas trade reached its nadir in the early nineteenth century and then underwent a great revival after Waterloo.

Ann Giffard and I have described part of Appledore's nineteenth century history in detail in *Westcountrymen in Prince Edward's Isle*. How Thomas Burnard, greatest of all Bideford's shipowners, sent the little *Peter & Sarah* to the Island in 1818 to put a party of local shipwrights ashore and establish a shipbuilding industry, how his nephew, Thomas Burnard Chanter, established a large timber importing and emigration business from the Torridge, and how the whole business was gradually acquired, and once acquired greatly expanded, by James Yeo, once the carrier from Kilkhampton to Bideford, who had gone to the Island to manage Thomas Burnard's lumbering gang and houses in 1819. James Yeo sent his eldest son, William, back to Appledore to be his British agent and James and William enclosed Appledore's sheltered bay and built the great Richmond Drydock where it had been. They also built Richmond House, now called The Holt, the great mansion at the top of the hill above the shipyards. Both house and dock were named for Richmond Bay, the source of vessels and timber in Prince Edward Island. In the drydock vessels built in the Island and sailed over were fitted out for selling in the British market. The business prospered mightily and James Yeo became the richest and most influential man in the Island.

Besides the site at East Appledore there was another shipbuilding place,

between Appledore and Irsha, down below the church, the Churchfield Yard.
Here Thomas Geen built vessels in the early nineteenth century and in 1850
the yard was taken over by William Cock, a member of a family which had
moved into Appledore from South Molton. A year later he died in one of the
periodic outbreaks of cholera which swept ill drained, insanitary, lawless and
overcrowded Appledore in the nineteenth century, but his family prospered
and when after the sudden death of William Yeo in 1872, only four years after
his father's death in Prince Edward Island, Appledore shipbuilding fell into a
depression it was Robert Cock, together with John Westacott of Barnstaple
who revived the industry, taking over the great yard James Yeo had established
between East Appledore and Bidna.

   The Cock family, by increasing the size of their enterprise and modernising
their methods kept the industry alive and prosperous when wood shipbuilding
was dying elsewhere in Britain. In the last ten years of the nineteenth century and the first thirteen of the twentieth a series of well designed schooners
was launched at Appledore and it was during this last period of prosperity for
small merchant sailing ships in Britain that W. J. Slade was learning his pro-
fession at sea. The successor to the Cock family was Philip Kelly Harris, a
Northam man who built up a considerable shipowning and shipbuilding
business early in the present century and whose sons, among them Mr. Fred
Harris of whom Mr. Slade speaks so highly in his narrative, steadily expanded
and modernised the shipyards. Today the old Yeo yard, now managed and
financed on modern lines, is famous all over the world for its modern ocean
going and harbour diesel towing craft and other specialised vessels.

   The development of Appledore reflected this shipbuilding history. The
groups of Georgian cottages were linked with groups of first Victorian and
then Edwardian houses. Fortunately those who built at this later period did
so with good taste and, as S. H. Burton has said in his book, *The North Devon
Coast*, the flavour of Appledore is still predominantly that of a village
"where the houses were built in the days when to build at all was to build
beautifully."

   In the nineteenth century the warren of small backstreets, the *drangs,*
which gives the place part of its distinctive character was developed. Some
of them are no more than narrow paths between the high blind sidewalls of
houses, leading to the courts on to which many cottages open. These courts,
and the cottages inside and out, are always fresh painted, or whitewashed, and
immaculately clean. A hundred years ago, or less, they had a certain vigorous
roughness and were not always so quiet and law abiding, or so friendly to the
stranger, as they are today. Many of the houses were little more than huts.
Indeed, throughout the nineteenth century Appledore was notorious for the
vigorous independence of its inhabitants and a lawlessness which was the

subject of periodic comment in the Devon press. The young Slade had many a lark in those alleyways. And in the cottages at night, with the unending mutter of the breakers on the bar always present as a fitting background, old stories of ghosts and witches and strange goings on were told. The belief in witchcraft and the supernatural was widespread. From his grandparents, the Hardings, who were born in the 1830s or early 40s the attentive boy heard it all. How a man scared a shipmate nearly to death by dressing himself in a sheet and snatching the other's hat as he walked under the churchyard wall. How his father, as a boy in the early 1870s, drew the blood of an alleged witch to break the curse she was believed to have put on the unsuccessful salmon boat in which he worked. He had to hide himself from her furious relatives for some time — but the boat caught fish on the next tide. With the stories of ghosts and great gales and the hard times of more than a hundred years ago, young Slade absorbed, too, something of the fierce nonconformity and the uncompromising conservatism of the place. But he was far too intelligent to absorb it uncritically, for he was not Alan Shaw's "bull of a sailor ...... for whom time measured only Meridians, and God was simply God."*

In 1840 the main streets of East Appledore were the present Market Street, Bude Street and Meeting Street. There was no Richmond Road, this came in 1856 with the Yeo's drydock and Richmond House. To enter Market Street by wheeled transport you went past Staddon and down Meeting Street or down Bude Street. You could enter Market Street on foot through the drang from the Strand which is still there. There was no Quay, but a cart track along the sands from the triangular bay where the drydock now is to Churchfield and Irsha. The houses on the south side of Market Street had yards or gardens with retaining walls built straight out of the foreshore, just as the houses on the seaward side of Irsha Street and the houses between the Bell Inn and the upper part of the shipyards do today. In 1844 the freeholders of Market Street, some of whom had private quays behind their back gardens, with encouragement from Thomas Chanter, who was then Lord of the Manor, finally linked them up into a continuous Quay outside their river walls. Then it became profitable to build little houses where the yards and gardens had been, their front doors opening on to what had now become Appledore Quay. Thus the Quay assumed the form familiar to W. J. Slade for the first forty-eight years of his life. It was a place of great character and charm, with the small sailing vessels lying alongside in their dozens, the seamen and boatmen in their long hand-knitted blue jerseys called frocks, the boys at work and

*Alan Shaw, "Joshua Slocum," in *May to Midsummer,* Outposts publications, Dulwich Village, 1958.

play among the boats out of school hours. Despite the fresh Atlantic winds the boys and girls were always bare footed. It was the custom to strip off shoes and socks as soon as the school gates were left behind, and of course some parents could not afford shoes and socks for their children for everyday use. The photographs show numerous puddles of rain on the old Quay and, as they were taken over a number of years, they perhaps belie those elderly men of Appledore in my own youth who would have it that summers were always long and smiling and the weather steadily predictable in those days.

But despite its charms the old Quay had grave disadvantages. It was just wide enough for a four-wheeled cart of the type with small front wheels which swivelled under the body to turn, and it was rough and potholed. When the first motor lorries came after the turn of the century Appledore mothers used to cry (as Vernon Boyle recorded in *Devon Harbours*), "Run cheeld, run! Put thy arse against the wall!" And the old Quay was regularly flooded on high spring tides, or when westerly gales piled up the two rivers inside the bar, to the considerable discomfort of those who lived and traded on it. Between 1938 and 1940 the Quay was greatly widened and raised. Between the wars many new houses were built up the hillsides, over at West Appledore and above the shipyards, and by the end of the period covered by Mr. Slade's story Appledore had assumed its present form.

The most apparent feature in the history and geography of Appledore has perhaps always been the famous bar, Bideford, Barnstaple or Appledore bar, the shallow sand across the channel where the joint stream of the Taw and the Torridge flows out into the sea. This bar, which makes the waterway difficult to enter and even more difficult to leave, features large in the reminiscences of any Appledore seaman. Because of it, the five shipping centres of Apple-dore, Bideford, Braunton, Barnstaple and Fremington, which lie within the bar, are often called the "bar ports" and the seamen of Appledore itself were known far and wide as "barmen". Those who sailed in local trade about the Bristol Channel were known in other ports as "Down Homers," perhaps because of some variations of the local expression "to get down along" meaning "to continue the voyage", which Mr. Slade uses more than once in his narrative.

Notice also how he uses the term "vessel" to mean a small sailing or auxiliary motor ship, preferably wooden, as opposed to a steamer or fully powered motor ship. I have heard the term used in exactly the same sense by schooner trained seamen in the north-eastern part of the United States, though they extend it to include the large many masted schooners which were developed there during Mr. Slade's childhood.

The sort of local shipowning in which W. J. Slade made his career began with the down home trade in small vessels in the eighteenth and early nineteenth centuries. Small cargo smacks carried goods to all the harbours of the Bristol Channel. The sea was the natural means of transport when roads were few and abominable. As industry and population developed there were at first more small cargoes to carry. The local trade received a great fillip when the extension of cultivation in North Devon and Somerset created a great demand for lime. Kilns were built at almost every point on the coast where a small vessel with a cargo of limestone from South Wales could be put ashore to be unloaded, sometimes by women, and the Report of the Census of 1851 for the Parish of Northam in which Appledore then lay has numerous references to women described as "limestone porters". The limestone trade was for many years the core of the "Down Homers' " business and there are many stories of it in the contemporary North Devon newspapers. A whole class of very small square rigged ships with a variation of the ancient polacca rig came into being at Appledore and many of them were engaged in the limestone trade to which they were peculiarly suited. The trade persisted in some forms and in the present century little Appledore smacks were still bringing pebbles for lime burning from the North Devon coast in over the bar.

But by the time of W. J. Slade's grandparents the smacks had become bigger. Capital was accumulating among the small coasting shipowners. The steady employment and high level of local economic activity provided by Thomas Chanter's enterprise and later and on a much larger scale by the fitting out of James Yeo's Canadian built vessels and his great North American timber and emigrant trade generated capital and increased the size of the seafaring population. The expansion of building in Bristol, Cardiff, Barry and Newport created a demand for gravel from the banks in the Torridge and the Taw. There was more business for the market boats to do carrying the goods of growing villages and small towns about the Bristol Channel. Bigger smacks took coal from Lydney in Gloucestershire to the sandy coves of Cornwall where they beached and unloaded into carts. This dangerous but lucrative trade continued until immediately before the second world war and Mr. Slade has something to say about it in his narrative. William Kingdon Slade, W. J. Slade's father, was born in 1865 and in his time the smacks were cut in half, dragged apart with horses, and new flat midships sections were built into them to lengthen them and increase their cargo capacity. Then they were re-rigged as ketches.

They traded on the third share system, described in Mr. Slade's first chapter, which was a great incentive to a master to work hard and efficiently. They kept their little shipowning groups within the family — the 64 shares into which vessel property was legally divided were distributed among brothers and cousins, aunts and nephews, a tight knit group which would work together in financial matters. Their crews were cheap. They paid their men

by the voyage and if they were Appledorians they were not fed when windbound in Appledore. They were experts on working the small ports where
costs to the vessel were low and they avoided the expensive ones. Many of
the vessels were maintained on a very low standard and would not be allowed
to sea today. Thus further capital was accumulated.

In the last thirty years of the nineteenth century numerous schooners and
ketches, tending steadily to become larger, were built or bought in over the
bar, and this process continued on a diminishing scale with larger vessels up
to and through the first world war. After the war capital was available for
the widespread adoption of auxiliary motors. The life was still very hard but
in three generations it had greatly changed for the better. The fourth
generation was born into very different conditions and quite rightly did not
accept the hard old fashioned life in small wooden motor sailing ships.
Ashore the long impending change from horses to petrol was already far
advanced and motor lorries took more and more of such small cargoes as
advancing industry left for the schooners and ketches. Later, given the
opening up of so many lucrative opportunities ashore, the capital readily
available was not sufficient to tempt the shipowning families to take the great
step to the construction of new steel fully powered motorships and events
were to prove them right in not taking this course.

The life of Appledore which had changed only very slowly during the past
seventy-five years now changed very rapidly out of all recognition. Now the
shipyards which were the complement of shipowning and seafaring for
generations have become the main support of the community, and their
function is the construction of new specialised tonnage for the great ports,
rather than the repair and maintenance of local vessels. There can be no
comparison between W. J. Slade's life and that of his children, let alone his
grandchildren. And Rosina Annie Abigail Harding, who went to sea with her
father and brothers in a coasting smack nearly a century ago and lived to see
the first edition of this book published saw a greater change in the way of life
and the standard of living of her community than anybody had ever been
able to see before in history.

With this change of world very old seaman's and boatman's arts and skills,
to which these schooner and ketch men of Appledore were among the last
heirs in Britain, have, of course, been lost. As they link us to the early days of
man's conquest of the sea, and as some comprehension of them helps towards
a greater understanding of much of our history, their loss is to be regretted.
Moreover, the later small sailing ships could be as beautiful, both in their hull
form and in their general appearance under sail, as most things man has
devised to help him raise his standard of living. But the Slades were great
innovators, with simpler and more efficient sail plans and happy combinations

of sail and diesel power. They would be the first to recognise that by no means all has been lost. The modern ocean racing and cruising yacht is much faster, more seaworthy, more efficient, than any small sailing vessel has ever been in the history of seafaring before. But she does not earn a hard living for an industrious community by carrying heavy cargoes. She cannot be maintained at low cost with the skills of seaman, carpenter and blacksmith.

The reader will wish to know what exactly I have done in making these selections for publication from Mr. Slade's narrative. I have, with Mr. Slade's agreement, chosen passages from the full manuscript, (which is over one hundred thousand words long), which we think to be of most importance and interest in presenting a shorter continuous narrative of Mr. Slade's life. The substantial omissions are indicated in the usual way by dots . . . . . .

There has been little or no editing of the original text. What is printed here,is, apart from one or two minor clarifications and some changes of punctuation, just what he wrote in a series of exercise books at his home in Bideford between 1954 and 1957. In order that the serious student shall have the whole narrative at his disposal we have deposited a typewritten copy of the original manuscript, exactly as it was written, in the Manuscripts collection at the National Maritime Museum.

A word about the photographic illustrations. They are all acknowledged. The splendid ones from the Fox Collection at the National Maritime Museum demand special explanation. Although they depict the background of Mr. Slade's early life so closely, indeed one of them probably shows the boy Slade at work on one of his grandfather's boats, he was quite unaware that they existed until he was asked to identify some of them fifty years after they were taken. They were made by Mr. Fox of Cardiff who with his wife and his son, W. C. Fox, spent many summers at Appledore in the early years of this century.

Mr. Slade and I wish to thank H. Oliver Hill for his endless encouragement and help in the preparation of this book.

BASIL GREENHILL

London and Bideford, 1970

INTRODUCTORY NOTE TO THE NEW EDITION

This book has established itself as one of the modern classics of maritime history. As it goes into its fourth edition, interest in the way of life it describes – quite remote from anything we know today – is perhaps greater than ever before. Three sailing vessels of the type in which Captain Slade spent his working life have been preserved by national institutions. The ketch *Shamrock,* jointly owned by The National Maritime Museum and the National Trust, is to be seen in her berth at Cotehele Quay in Cornwall restored exactly as she was in 1926. The ketch *Garlandstone*, now the property of the National Museum of Wales, is preserved at Porthmadog. The steel schooner *Result* is now owned by the Ulster Folk Museum. In addition, the schooner *Kathleen & May* has been preserved by The Maritime Trust and can be seen in St Katharine's Dock in London.

The National Maritime Museum has opened galleries illustrating the history of small merchant sailing vessels before the First World War at Greenwich (Gallery 13) and at its Cotehele outpost. A local maritime museum has been established at Appledore by the North Devon Museum Trust. Captain Slade himself has published in *Westcountry Coasting Ketches* a very valuable detailed record of the ketch-rigged merchant sailing vessels of Appledore and the south-west of England. Many other books of local maritime history have followed the first publication of *Out of Appledore*, but it stands today, as it did when Captain Slade wrote it in the 1950s, as a unique firsthand account of life in a seafaring and small shipowning family on the way up in rural Britain before the great divide of the First World War.

Basil Greenhill
Greenwich, 1980

CHAPTER I

HOW IT ALL BEGAN

I HAVE BEEN asked to set down in writing a short history of how my family first started as owners of small coastal ketches and schooners and of my own life at sea. To do this I have to go back a generation or two, long before I made my entry into a life that was hard, but nevertheless had its compensations and even pleasures, in a limited manner.

My grandfather was one of a seafaring family. His brothers, I have heard, were at one time in the " hard case " yankee square riggers and were both drowned at sea whilst serving as mates. My grandfather, however, was illiterate, and he spent years as bosun in square rigged ships running to Quebec, and other North American ports. On some of these voyages the return trip would take him to Bristol, where he met his future wife. He must have been deeply in love with her because he walked from Appledore to Bristol to see her, in those days when no land transport was available that he could afford.

They married and in due course settled at Appledore. Grandfather had a voice like a roaring lion, but underneath he was an easygoing, lovable character with a heart of gold. Grandmother's people came from South Molton; her maiden name was Elizabeth Kingdon; some of her connections still live there, I believe. She never took poverty lying down, she was a born leader, and ruled her numerous offspring like a queen. Her word was law till she died and no one dared to contradict or answer her back when she gave an order, but she was deeply loved and respected by all. She had 15 children. Her eldest son, who died when he was about 30, was master of a small ketch trading from the Bristol Channel to the Cornish ports and beaches.

After he had made several more deepwater trips, my grandmother insisted on keeping her husband at home. A few fishing boats were purchased and she set out to wrest a living from the rivers Taw and Torridge, the two rivers of North Devon which flow out into the sea at Appledore through a common mouth. She put her children to work in those boats with her husband as soon as they were big enough. She found her own markets through her London relatives and gradually got a business going whereby she not only sold her own fish, but was agent for others as well. Every penny went through her hands and it wasn't long before she bought her own house. As the sons reached the age of 16 or 17 they went to sea, and, having had a hard existence on the water from early childhood, they one and all took to it quickly. They were not exactly greenhorns because it was part of their work to sail schooners in and out over Bideford Bar, with their father as pilot, and they got a knowledge of our bar and harbour that was wonderful.

My father's first ship was a brigantine. Father was an ordinary seaman and in those days he was quiet and rather shy. The mate was a " hard case," a bully and very unpleasant to live with. One morning while the ship was lying in the Downs windbound, the mate came on deck and accused the ordinary seaman of stealing his cravat. If there was anything my grandmother hated, it was dishonesty and she taught her children to be honest above all things. Naturally the accusation was indignantly denied and in a second the mate struck my father, knocking him flat. Now Father had spent a lot of time in his boyhood being taught self-defence by his grandparent on his mother's side. He recovered himself after a few moments and then a fight took place which ended only when the captain interfered to save the mate from being badly hurt. That mate had a lesson he didn't want repeated, but it made Father very unhappy. He was unable to write, but his mother could, and in due course she wrote, sending an envelope addressed to herself. Her letter enquired how he was going on. He replied filling up a sheet of paper with " V.B., V.B., V.B." She ordered him home, and he obeyed and left the brigantine.

Sometime during this period my father's eldest sister, Mary Ann Slade, married a deep water sailor, George Quance, who was a clever man. He could do anything with a piece of wire or rope, carve or paint pictures, or make a sail. Despite these gifts, during the first few years my aunt had very little to be proud of in her marriage. But she was a woman who had a great personality and had a wonderful influence in shaping the future of both her husband and herself. I may say she started my family in small ship-owning. My uncle gave up sailing in the tea clippers and went on the coast as mate of the brigantine *Danube* and Father sailed with him. After a year or two my uncle became master of a ketch called the *George Cannon*.

During these years Aunt Mary Ann worked hard for a living as a dressmaker. It was her practice to go to anyone's house to work. She would sew all day at her machine for a certain fee and have her meals free. She also took in work and would stay up often all night to get her dressmaking orders done. In this way she earned sufficient cash to keep her home going without ever needing to touch a penny of her husband's earnings. She worked and saved enough to buy a small ketch called the *Nouvelle Marie* for her husband.

It was a great shock to Uncle George when his wife told him what she was in a position to do. He determined to back her up and he certainly did so. It was a very successful beginning which bore a rich harvest in the course of some years. After being some considerable time in a square rigged ship Father was appointed master of another ketch called the *Francis Beddoe* which was owned by Phillip Kelly Harris, the founder of the Appledore shipbuilding firm. I think he also sailed one voyage in the Cunarder *Umbria* before returning to the coastal trade. Another brother went into the deepwater foreign trade for a period, and also returned to the coast as master of a small vessel. Thus they all succeeded in their various jobs and settled down in the home trade, having married and made homes for themselves.

The next step was the purchase of a 100 ton ketch called *Heather Bell*. This was a very strong ship, built at Barnstaple as a schooner and belonging to the Isle of Man. She went ashore on the South Tail of Bideford Bar and hammered her way in over until she fell into deep water. She was offered for sale at Appledore and was purchased in her damaged condition by my father and his mother. Uncle Tom took charge of her as master. It was found there was practically no damage and no floors were broken. She went to sea and there is no doubt Uncle Tom did a remarkable lot of work with her. She was indeed a fine bargain and a money spinner for all those interested in her.

The brothers and family worked very hard, always sticking together in business, although often having their differences. Then along came a schooner called *Alpha* (Plate 1) which was purchased by the family. My father became master of this lovely little ship and she was another success. Father used to say she was a little gold mine. She was built by Charles Dyer at Sunny Corner, halfway between Truro and Malpas in Cornwall, and her hull was so fine that there was nowhere on her planking that a two foot rule would touch throughout its length. Father used to say that her gaffs were so light that they could be carried each by one man on his shoulder.

Through these three ships, *Nouvelle Marie, Heather Bell* and *Alpha*, all the male members of the family were supplied with a ship and some more ships were also purchased for men outside the family. The secret of their success was family co-operation. The ships were sailed on the third share system. This gave the owners one-third, out of which they paid all insurances and upkeep of ship's gear. The other two-thirds of the ship's freight belonged to the master out of which he paid the wages, food and all port expenses. Any balance was his own, and was considered his wages. The master made many voyages without pay, but sometimes he did quite well. If he did well for himself by making extra trips, the owners also did well, but it can readily be understood that the master, who also did the chartering, got the biggest freight and kept clear of the big expensive ports whenever possible. He sailed without pilots and worked all cargoes with the crew. Through the years down to my own life at sea twenty-two ships of different rigs and sizes were bought by the family. Commander Hill has given the history of each of them in the first Appendix to this book. It was what was left of the ship's share after the payment of insurance and upkeep, always allowed to accumulate and never spent, that bought other ships.

My father married Rosina Annie Abigail Harding, a sailor's daughter who had three brothers. All were brought up in a deeply religious atmosphere and mother sailed with her father and brothers on many voyages in their cargo smack the *Dahlia,* and other vessels. She was therefore an ideal wife for a coasting master, being able to take her turns at the wheel. She knew quite a lot about a ship, but, best of all, by the standards of those days she was a good scholar. It wasn't very long after he was married that father was able to write simple letters to her. He had had a very hard life as a boy, he never went to school and his hard upbringing gave him a hard outlook on life. After marriage he never rested, working night and day until he bought his own home, in Westcroft Terrace, Irsha Street, West Appledore. Mother did all his business for him, but being more or less illiterate was always a great handicap to him.

I was the eldest son in a family of ten. When I made my first appearance in the world on April 28, 1892, it was blowing a north west gale, fishing boats sank at their moorings and Father came in over the bar to find he had a son, so that my birth was indeed a stormy entry into life. Mother took me to sea the following summer and from then the sea became my heritage. I was taken to school at the age of three but always spent a month at sea every year. I knew every sail at an early age and how they were set. To handle a small boat came like learning to walk. When at sea I loved to keep the first watch with Father and would eagerly listen to his experiences, especially how he survived the blizzard of March, 1891, off the Cornish Coast and his terrible hardship alone on the deck of the *Francis Beddoe* for four days and nights; and I would also love to hear him sing " Tom Bowling," " Larbord Watch," etc. It didn't matter to me that all the songs had the same tune, they were so romantic to my young ears.

On one particular voyage to Waterford in the *Alpha* we were short-handed. Mother and I were on the quarter deck, when passing the Smalls in a strong northerly wind. The salt spray was flying about and we both got wet. Father laughed and said, " That's nothing. I'll be in Waterford Harbour tonight." Mother replied, " If you carry the topsail like this, you'll lose your topmast." She was right, for there was a sudden crash and down it all came. I was put below and Mother went on deck to look after the ship, while Father went aloft to help clear the wreckage. It sounded like hell let loose for half an hour, but I had to stay below and was not allowed on deck again till we were entering Waterford Harbour. Mother didn't half pull Father's leg over this, but he took it all in good part. In fact Mother was the only person in the world who could handle him properly. I never saw him laugh heartily. I did see him try once over something she said, when he was drinking tea and he nearly choked, but Mother was full of fun and she would nearly split her sides laughing at him.

We had a new topmast made at Waterford and loaded timber for Cardiff. From Cardiff we sailed to Lydney in Gloucestershire.

Going up the Severn we had to race for " stem "; the first off the
pier loaded first. The water over Lydney grounds was doubtful.
Our ship was empty and rather crank, so our topsail was carried
to the last minute to keep her down on her side. As soon as she
was over the shallow part it was " down topsail," quick. I was
stationed at the halliards to let go when the order came. I did it
all right but I caught my fingers in the block and let out a yell.
I had bungled the job and I got no sympathy from Father for my
squeezed fingers. I never caught them again; it was too painful
to repeat.

The cargo on that occasion was for Mevagissey in Cornwall.
When we arrived the fishing was having a boom and we couldn't
get men to work the cargo, so I was set to work on the winch,
Father on one winch handle and I on the other. In order to raise
me high enough a booby hatch was placed for me to stand on,
and Father kept me at it by continually shouting. I was only
eight and a half years of age and I'm afraid it was hard work for
Father. I did my best and probably helped him a little bit, but I
was being trained for future use. When the cargo was out, I
received one shilling. It was a small fortune to me in those days.
That night it was early to bed as I was needed to help get under
way in the early hours of the morning, but I slept till the next
afternoon and when I did wake up and got on deck we were
beating down across Mounts Bay. Up to that time I had not
been sea sick. I don't know why it started but for the rest of my
life afterwards I was never completely free of it.

In due course we arrived at Appledore and I had to go to school
and was not allowed to go to sea again until the following summer.
In the meantime I was a source of worry to my grandfather. I
used to unmoor his boat and go out in the river. There were
generally two or three of his grandsons (Plate 4) and we used to
set the foresail without the sprit. It wasn't dangerous as long as
we kept the sprit down, but it wasn't long before we got it up and
then the fun began. Grandfather would find out and he would
roar like a lion and threaten to give us his straps, but we knew
he wouldn't actually do it. It was all bark, but not bite, and he
was really a dear old chap and quite harmless. During the winter
my father would make a few short voyages to Fremington and I
was always kept home from school to go on board whenever the
ship came in over the bar. In getting up the river to Fremington
kedge anchors were often used for the last half mile and my father

used to say the boy was handy to hold the rope on the winch when the men were heaving on the handles, and woe betide me if I let it slip out of my hands when it surged on the winch end.

And so life went on until I was eleven. One day our schoolmaster gave out that any boy could take an examination to leave school provided he was over twelve. This examination took place on April 30th and my twelfth birthday fell on the 28th of April so I was only just eligible. I was the youngest of sixty boys from Bideford and district to take part. Nine passed including three from Appledore and I was one of those three. This was indeed one of the milestones of my life, which I have often regretted.

As soon as I knew I was entitled to leave school, I did so. Mother was away and I was a free agent. It was all done without my parents' knowledge and when Father got the news he came home from Teignmouth and my bag was packed to join his ship, now the ketch *Ulelia*, another beautiful model of a vessel built, like the *Alpha*, by Charles Dyer at Sunny Corner, near Truro, as a member of the crew for the first time. I was allowed one shilling per voyage for pocket money and it was no use asking for a rise.

On the first voyage we loaded ball clay for Cork and, in addition to my cooking, which I had to learn, cleaning brasswork, scrubbing out cabin and galley *after hours*, my job on the cargo was to slide the square balls of clay from the ship's rail in over the hatch combings to the hold. This wasn't hard work, but I had to do it and it would become irksome before the day ended.

In due course we sailed. After passing the Longships we encountered a strong north westerly wind and I became very sea sick. I wasn't much good that trip. One morning the head earing of the mainsail parted. The able seaman was a good man. He cut off a length of new line and was soon going out over the peak halliards to fix a new one. This was something new to me and I was afraid he would be thrown off the gaff end. I forgot seasickness till he was safely on deck, but with no food and days of sickness I finally gave up and crawled into my bunk, wishing to die and get it over quickly. I think Father must have foreseen trouble with me. A bottle of brandy appeared and I was given an occasional tot to keep me going. I did my best to keep it down, but sometimes the inevitable happened and Father would call me lots of names that I wasn't given when I was christened, for wasting good spirits.

One morning I was called up to see the Irish coast in sight.

The wind had backed south west and we were under single reefs. There was a nasty sea, but I suddenly felt hungry and I was soon helping myself to bread and butter. By the time we reached Cork I was alive and kicking.

One day in Cork I was late getting the dinner and had a severe reprimand from Father. I sulked from my meal but I soon realised that didn't cut any ice. When I got too hungry, I wanted to eat, but Father said, " The dinner hour is from one till two o'clock." and I was kept till knock off time, 6 p.m., before I had a bite of food. I never sulked again. It didn't pay me. Those five hours were agony. That night I had orders to scrub out the cabin and all hands went ashore. I felt pretty miserable. To add to my troubles a steamer came under the stern and with violently working her propeller our stern ropes parted and off we went. Some men started shouting, " Let go the anchor." It was very dark but I managed to drop it on the ground to keep the ship quiet till Father came with the crew. Of course I got some praise for that and all my past sins and omissions were wiped out.

We got in some short trips on the Irish coast with general cargo. Finally, some time after, we loaded at Cork for Barnstaple. We sailed from Cork and my spirits rose high at the prospect of being home for Sunday, but I didn't bargain for what I should have to suffer before we reached our destination. We sailed on a Friday evening with a light south westerly wind, heading for Lundy Island. On Saturday afternoon we started reefing. It soon became apparent we were in for a blow. The craft was pretty deeply laden. Father would never go short of cargo if he could help it and it was always understood when carrying manure, as we were this time, that the bags were extra weight, carried for nothing. The wind freshened to a gale and we were shipping water on deck, fairly heavy at times. I was sent below and kept there sitting in the cabin by the fire and fairly comfortable, often getting up to look out of the side of the skylight. I heard them saying Lundy was sighted right ahead. The sea had now become very heavy. It seemed as if an earthquake suddenly struck her. The top of the skylight lifted, the cabin was plunged in darkness by water streaming down. The cabin lamp was out, the fire washed out and I stood up to my knees in water, smothered in steam and dust from the fireplace. There seemed to be dead silence on deck and for a moment I thought they were all washed overboard, and I felt like a rat in a trap.

I had to get fresh air. I suddenly remembered there were two doors in the companion. They were on slides. I got the inner one back and reached in the recess for the outer one. I opened it, pushed my head through, and yelled, " Let me out."

Someone answered, " It's the boy. There's something wrong down there." When they opened up, the steam came up, and they saw the water washing about. The ship was now hove to and not shipping so much. They opened up the lazarette board and let the water down so that the cabin was clear. I wanted to stay on deck, but I was shut down again and I had a most uncomfortable night. I asked the mate if we should soon be inside Lundy, just before he left me. His reply was not very diplomatic. I was told we should never get in anywhere. But I remember Father's yarns about the blizzard and I had complete faith in his ability to see us through. I was still too young to realise the power of the elements. All I knew was that my father was on deck, and although I feared him, I also trusted him implicitly.

The next morning I was told to come on deck. The wind had veered north west. We were inside Lundy running into Bideford Bay and the decks were a proper shambles. Ropes and bower chains were tangled up in the lee scuppers, some were out through the wash ports towing behind. We were heading for the bar and Father lashed me to the mainrail on the weather quarter in case she shipped a heavy sea while crossing the bar. The crew cleared the decks, got everything ready for entering, and we soon got into smooth water and safety. After we moored at Appledore, the pumps were attended to and Father was afraid the cargo might be damaged, so he had to make a protest at the public notary in order to cover himself from any claim.

When we got ashore Mother made a great fuss. She knew all about the weather. She suggested I should stay ashore and finish with the sea. I knew Father was watching my reaction to this and I wasn't going to show the white feather even if I was a bit cheesed off, so I refused to stay home and I was a hero for a short time. I wallowed in this praise, of course, but underneath I knew I wasn't such a fine chap as I tried to appear; but I also felt how easy it was to make them believe something if they wanted to. . . .

Well, to return to my life at sea, nothing unusual occurred for some time. We continued in the coasting trade and I was learning fast. I had to read all the business letters and often, when I expected a quiet sit down, I would be called to the cabin to write

a dozen or so postcards and letters to get charters for further
cargoes. There was always writing to do and if Father wasn't
good at writing it was surprising how he could dictate. I hated
the job, but it was certainly good for me. It taught me what
business was and gave me a thoroughly good knowledge. Even
as a small boy I had to do the deeds of transfer if we bought or
sold a ship; and all ship's papers, customs business, etc., went
through my hands. There was also a lot of figuring to do when
we carried grain, slates and other stuff. It all came my way and I
managed to satisfy in this respect, if not in other ways.

One voyage on the way back from the Fastnet we found ourselves
in the upper part of Bude Bay. It had been dirty foggy weather
and we were becalmed close in to Sharpnose. The weather looked
black and threatening and we hadn't got too much ballast in the
bottom. Suddenly we were struck by a north west gale. All hands
were standing by and the sails were let down very smartly. It had
to be done quickly. The vessel went over on her bulwarks with a
lee shore and treacherous rocks close to us. Father put his arm
round me and his words were full of affection and tragedy, " You'll
never see Mother again." It sounded pretty grim, but I still
remembered Father's stories of his experiences, and, strange as it
may seem, I was not afraid. I once again trusted him and once
again he proved himself a man. The ship seemed to recover
somewhat after the first gust had struck her and Father leaped
into action like a tiger. The crew responded to his orders in quick
time. The first order came, " Set the fore staysail ! "

This was done and the mate came back aft evidently badly
scared, but he didn't have a chance to think. The next order was,
" Shake a reef out of the mainsail," and I can remember everything seemed to be straining to bursting point. The lee mainrail
was in the water and Hartland light close under the lee bow.

" Shake a reef out of the mizzen and jump to it. It's neck or
nothing." I was doing all I could to help, holding on the halliards
under the pins while they sweated it up. Nobody bothered about
water : I only know I was waist-deep in it, till the job was done.
Father stood at the wheel, his teeth clenched. How she stood that
battering I have never understood, but just as they thought it was
impossible to weather the Tings (a reef of rocks off Hartland) she
seemed to creep to windward and she did clear, but I afterwards
understood it was by an alarmingly small margin, and only the
fact that she took the ebb tide under the lee bow in the last moments

Plate 1.   *W. J. Slade*
    The ketch *Alpha*, built near Truro in Cornwall, which was purchased by the
Slade family in 1897.

Plate 2. *W. J. Slade*
W. J. Slade's father, William Kingdon Slade, at about the time of his marriage.

Plate 3. *W. J. Slade*
W. J. Slade's mother, Rosina Annie Abigail Harding, from a photograph taken at the same time as that of her husband in Plate 2.

Plate 4. *National Maritime Museum*
Although positive identification is impossible, after fifty years, it seems almost certain that these three small boys on the hard below Appledore Quay are the cousins, W. J. Slade (left), Thomas Slade (centre) and Richard Slade (right) working on one of their grandfather's boats. All became successful shipmasters and owners.

saved her from smashing to pieces on the rocks which would have been inevitable death to every one of us. The next morning was Sunday and we ran in over the bar to Appledore. The weather moderated and we sailed again on Monday.

Now it happened that during the previous Saturday night I had been wearing Father's shoes and of course they got soaking wet. I hadn't dried them and he found them unfit to put on. He forgot all about Saturday night's demonstration of affection, but I didn't forget what I got for getting his shoes wet. I had used them without his knowledge and I had to pay for it, which I suppose was only justice.

Life in those early days was certainly no bed of roses. When at sea I was often miserably seasick and as Father never felt seasick in his life he had no sympathy for me and perhaps it was just as well. When we got in harbour, the cargo had to be winched out and I had to do my full share. In addition, when the others had their rest between meals, there was always something for me to do. The daily routine was : get up 6 a.m., light the fire and get breakfast going, then on the winch. If there was a minute to spare, run into the galley, see to the fire, etc. ; 8 a.m. take the breakfast down for the crew. After breakfast the others had a rest, but not the boy: he washed up dishes and cleared away the mess, hurriedly got the dinner going and then the shouting commenced. " Come on, slowcoach, it's time to start work. They are waiting for you." At dinner time the same thing again. After tea the crew had their freedom, but the boy still had a lot to do. The stove had to be cleaned out, the fire laid in ready for the morning and the potatoes had to be peeled for dinner the next day. It was always 9 p.m. before the boy finished work and after a wash it was time to go to bed. How I longed to be promoted to ordinary seaman !

The day came when I did get a chance, but it wasn't a real one. In fact it led to harder work and no relief from my former job. Indeed my eagerness was never rewarded in the way I expected. When I was the bottom dog, I was told it was my place to stay on board and look after the ship. When I became an able seaman, it was still my duty and if anything went wrong in Father's absence the blame was laid on me. When I finally became mate, I still carried the responsibility. Although we were only coasting it was not uncommon for me to be three months on board without any freedom to go ashore enjoying myself. I think this was really good for me, as I was kept away from the riotous behaviour usually associated with the sailor ashore. Indeed there was no money to spend in any case, although Father often brought me a free bar of chocolate and I was fond of that. . . .

After making a few more trips we were lying at Appledore loaded with clay for Liverpool. It was found our mast coat needed to be renewed. When it was lifted, it was with dismay we discovered the mast was rotten in the deck. We lifted the mizzen coat and that mast was also gone. To deal with this at once meant discharging our cargo again. Father refused to face this expense, so it was decided that Messrs. R. Cock, who were then shipbuilders at Appledore, should get the necessary baulks of pitchpine to make the masts and that we should make our voyage to the Mersey and back. It was also arranged to give the ship new topsides and all new decks. This was going to be a long job and I looked forward to a nice holiday, which, however, didn't come off.

On our voyage we were in company with another local ship. It came on to a strong wind and being rather afraid of our mast we reduced our sail more than usual. There were few, if any, ships on the coast that would equal ours in speed, but this time we were beaten and Father had to listen to jibes from the crew of the other ship, which didn't improve his temper and I kept clear whenever possible. He dared not tell anyone about the two masts as it was possible we might be stopped by the Board of Trade if it became known. However, we got home safely and went into dry dock. I had five or six weeks' hard scraping the ship from keel to gunwale, tarring, painting and helping in the unrigging and re-rigging of our craft. The old mizzen mast made a standing bowsprit so it was all new, and we were classed A1 at Lloyd's for six years in black when we finished. For all this I received no pay and I was glad to get a few coppers in various ways unknown to Father. I sold many buckets of old iron bolts and bits of old rope that I gathered up. In this way I kept my pockets going in a quiet and humble way.

The jib-boom and bowsprit which we had previously had were condemned because we were always in trouble with the harbour-master at Lydney. We were forced to get the jib-boom in often, but we always sailed up and down the River Severn and it was an awful lot of trouble to slack up the head stays, guys and back ropes, besides it was extremely awkward to be pushed out in a dangerous river with the ship half rigged, perhaps with a strong wind and little room to move. The jib-boom had to be got out and all stays set up between tacking and the very necessary headsails could not be set until this was done.

Father took an oath one day that he'd never take the jib-boom in again, so when the next time came, we sailed to the pier at Lydney boldly. The harbour-master shouted orders, " Get your jib-boom in." Father shouted back, " It's impossible, I've had to bolt the jib-boom and bowsprit together." The excuse was accepted. It was certainly made to look genuine, as if the guy had carried away with a northerly wind coming up Channel. Part of the step where the heel of the jib-boom fitted was split off and a bolt was driven down through the heel but the bolt only just penetrated an inch into the bowsprit. So we were all satisfied and that was the end of what was certainly an awkward job in narrow waters, until we had a standing bowsprit fitted and there was no further necessity to deceive anyone.

When we left Appledore bound for Liverpool with clay again, after our heavy repairs, we had a new mate. He was the best man I had ever had as a shipmate. He had been in the North Sea sailing trawlers belonging to Lowestoft as a young man and had married and settled in Appledore. From the outset he was good to me and I responded to his kindness by doing all I could to please. If a sail wanted repairs a palm and needle was passed to me and if the rigging and gear wanted overhauling he would join with me in preparing our food first and then we'd work together and he taught me a lot I never knew before. He made me an able seaman and I was happier than I'd ever been. . . .

As I had also learnt quite a lot in coastal navigation, I was trusted in this department absolutely. Many times when we were at sea out of sight of land for days and I would be a little seasick, I would have orders, " Get out the chart and tell me the exact position of the vessel." Of course I had to obey. It was really done to take my mind off the sickness, but it paid dividends. I was taught the tidal currents and how they set at different states of the tide, how to allow for the set, cross bearings, four point bearings and a host of other things. I kept a pocket book for years and everything I was told went down in that little book till I could memorise it properly. On one trip from Aberdovey to Heybridge Basin (Maldon) and from there to Woolwich Buoys, where we loaded oilcake for Barnstaple, I was told to take the ship and find my way. Father had never been to Maldon and I gave all the navigation orders, going in over part of London flats and next morning through the Swin till we arrived. I made a good job of it and for a lad of sixteen deserved praise, but I didn't get a word either way. Indeed, I found out only by accident some time afterwards that Father was very proud of the education he was giving me. . . .

In fact I had got to the point when I realised I was indispensable to Father. My mother had dropped out of the business part and everything in the way of accounts and chartering went through my hands. Father had learnt to lean on me in every direction. It had come gradually and no one noticed it. Life got a little easier after this and the work more equally distributed, but it was still hard. Whenever we left the Irish side to go to Lydney there was always fifteen to twenty tons of ballast to get rid of. Sometimes it consisted of earth and old ruins of houses and this used to go solid after a day or two. We were in the habit of throwing it overboard anywhere between Barry and Kingroad and generally in the dark hours because, I understand, it was an offence to throw it out in the fairway. We used to anchor at high water, lower the sails, get up the discharging gear and then one hand would do the shovelling in the hold, two on the hand winch. When the basket was high enough one would leave the winch to tip it over the side. It would take us about three or four hours to get the ballast out and then if there was a couple of hours to spare before getting under way, I was always told off to keep the anchor watch and call the others at a given time. It would be arranged that I would have my nap after the anchor was up and the ship under way. That often was a promise that couldn't be carried out. Something often turned up to stop it, such as no wind, or fog. In the former case the anchor would be lifted and we'd go on drift, always standing by to drop it and heave up again. In fog all hands had to keep a look out. This practice, in my opinion, of taking advantage of the boy or third hand was common in all the Bideford sailing vessels in those days. The boy had the hardest job of all and if any of the older generation were asked to confirm this I'm quite sure the answer would be in the affirmative. . . .

One voyage soon after, we took linseed to Gloucester and from there went to Ramsgate with a cargo of salt. We shifted to London empty and loaded cement back to Gloucester. The weather was boisterous on the voyage back but being summer time we didn't go in windbound. It wasn't too bad, just uncomfortable. The wind had been fresh south west. We got inside the race off Portland, intending to have a night in Portland. It was dark as we were getting well down towards Portland when the wind veered north west. Father couldn't resist the chance to get down along, but when we opened out Portland, it was more than we bargained for. The gaff topsail had to be taken in and I was sent up to furl it. It happened to be the port side which was the lee side. I never had such a hard job in my life. I got on top of it to ride it down, but the ship was springing like a bucking bronco. It was awful until I managed to get a turn of the upper gasket round the eyes of the rigging. I really needed help but none came and I grumbled again when I had finished and got down on deck. No notice was taken until the next morning when it was seen my fingers were bandaged and Father wanted to know what it was for and I showed him how much skin was off my knuckles. He said that it would grow again but he admitted it was a tough job.

We got round the Longships and off Pendeen with a fresh northerly wind the head of the mainsail split. We were in company with several Brixham sailing trawlers on their way to the Lundy fishing ground. We had to put her head off and lower the mainsail down. It took about an hour to repair with every-body joining in and the wheel lashed. We got it up with one roll in and the gaff topsail set over it. We hove her round on the port tack and drove her hard up the Channel. About midnight we fetched in just below Trevose, and went about for a tack off the land again. The next morning we weathered Hartland and we were still in company with the trawlers. We were soon up above the Bull in finer weather and I was thankful that we were once more nearing the end of our journey, even if it did mean work and discharging and loading cargo.

There was no holiday at sea or in harbour, but I was soon to get promotion and a rise of 1s. 6d. a voyage. Father bought a schooner and I was told I had to join her at Garston as mate. She was a nice little craft, the *Elizabeth Jane*, built at Connah's Quay, Chester, carrying about 170 tons. She was two masted with topsail and flying topgallant sail. We loaded for Bideford and I felt happier than I had ever felt in all my previous years at sea, although it was a bit strange at first. After a day or so I began to feel quite at home and it seemed easier to handle the square topsails than to ride down a 90 or 100 yards gaff topsail single handed. I had yet to learn something when it came to beating a schooner over Liverpool Bar in a fresh wind, but Father very

C

soon drove his lessons home to me in his way, which was not very
gentle at any time. When we got out clear of the Bar the wind
freshened and blew hard about west south west and we had to take
in our topgallant sail and reef our mainsail. Being short handed
we had not found it easy to swing the yards round in stays, but
it was good practice and I think I was pretty quick on the uptake
in those days. After becketing the topgallant sail I stood on the
masthead and thought it was all wonderful. The ship was so
easy in her movements and we had two men to stow the sail. It
was just heaven in comparison with a large gaff topsail which I
was always handling alone under any conditions.

That night I took the first watch alone. I was so proud to know
I was trusted, that I was determined to prove I could sail a schooner
as well as a ketch. The night passed without any trouble and
Father was unusually good tempered, mainly because he found
she was tight, staunch, and strong, a fine little sea boat indeed,
and a bargain. The next morning we were on the port tack with
squally weather when the wind suddenly veered to a northerly
point. We put her on the starboard tack and shortly afterwards saw
the Skerries under the lee. We set our topgallant and then were
ordered to slack the lee braces and pull in the weather ones. Now
instead of slacking just a few feet I let them go altogether and
jumped across to the weather side to help. It was just touch and
go they didn't come all aback and I not only received a lesson
but it seemed to me all the world heard what Father said. It was
blowing hard but his voice was worse than all the foghorns on the
North Wales coast. What he said sank into my brain and my
pride suffered a heavy blow from which I took a long time to
recover.

After this I got on fine and we were soon home. Now our
insurance society at Braunton was informed by an unknown
friend that Father was sailing the *Elizabeth Jane* with a boy of 17
for mate. The club objected and I had to sit down and write a
letter to the effect that Father would agree to my being subjected
to any examination they wished to put me through and he would
guarantee me to pass with no difficulty.

The years I had put in at sea from the age of 12, plus the teaching
I had received in the years before I reached that age were mentioned
and also what Father considered I was capable of doing in
navigating a schooner on the coast. Practically all the members
of the committee were retired masters of coastal sailing ships and

most of them knew my record. The result of all this ended with my acceptance as mate without any further trouble. I was soon to be well tried.

We made a voyage or two to the Irish ports and on one of these loaded timber for Newport, Monmouthshire. We got above the Monkstone and ran for Newport river. It was a wild dirty night and blowing very hard south west. We were carrying too much mainsail. On going round the bend in the upper part of Bridg-waterman's Reach the mainsail jibed without warning and as quick as lightning I jumped to gather in some of the mainsheet to avoid damage. In doing so I saved certain damage to the gear but my leg got in a bight of the mainsheet and up I went in the bull's-eye. I brought up the weight of a forty feet main boom with my leg and let out a yell of pain. Father shouted, " Oh my poor boy. Billie, are you all right ? " I answered, " Yes, I'm all right," and before I could say another word, he tore into me like a raging hurricane. I can't remember the words, but it seemed very funny to be a darling boy one second and the next second an unprintable set of names I was never christened. Fortunately for me I had on leather sea boots, and, as my leg was out of action and I was in agony, I had to take the wheel and obey instructions while Father went forward to take in the sails. I was very glad when the anchor dropped outside the old dock. I had to get around the deck with the help of a broom which acted as a crutch. When the ship was in the Locks a police officer came on board to have a look at my leg and the sea boot had to be cut off through the leg being swollen up badly. It was found no bones were broken but my leg was black and bruised from ankle to knee. It was suggested I wasn't fit to carry on work as I could not stand on it, but this didn't suit Father. We were still short handed too and he had to employ a man to sling the timber in the hold in my place, which didn't improve the situation for me. It was six weeks before I put my foot on the deck again, but I had to work just the same and I got used to it in time. . . .

On one occasion soon after, while the *Elizabeth Jane* was lying on the mud at Crosspark, Bideford, I got up early in the morning to walk to Bideford from Appledore to go on board and help with tarring the ship. The idea was ' early to work and early knock off.' Being at home we liked to finish early. As usual I wasn't very presentable at the end of the day, so thought I'd go home over the river bank. I hadn't gone far when two young ladies approached. I recognised one of them: she was our local Baptist minister's daughter and I felt ashamed and very embarrassed, so went into the hedge to cut a small stick, but a voice said " Hello, Will." I pretended not to hear and with a guilty conscience passed on. I married her some years later.

When I got home, I put on my tidy suit and asked Mother for some money. She said, " Father is on the Quay, ask him. He'll give you some." I found him talking to another skipper and I tried him, thinking he was bound to come up trumps in company; but instead I was told to go on board, " Your knock off time is 6 p.m." But that time I didn't go. I had no money to spend, which after all was as usual, I didn't smoke, I didn't take intoxicating liquor, in fact I lived an exemplary life because, " needs must, when the devil drives ". . . .

Once we were bound to Porthello (Porthallow), an open beach situated between Porthoustock and Helford River, and our ship was too big for that place, which was frequented by small ketches and barges sometimes in summer, but I never knew of a schooner of 11 ft. 6 in. draft to go there. We had a big freight and if we got away with it Father would pocket a nice bit of money, and that counted volumes. We got up above the Manacles and it was decided to stick right in on the beach. This was fairly steep so we freed up about two feet going in with a good speed. The boat was got out at once and Father went ashore and arranged to start working cargo immediately. We stowed the sails and got up our discharging gear and by the time this was done the tide had ebbed sufficiently to enable the carts to back out under the bow up to axles in water. We managed to have a snack and the cargo was started. We worked till the tide came in and then moored the ship with stream anchors aft and to a post ashore for bow moorings. We had a meal and a wash, hove the vessel further in and went to bed. We had hardly got time to go off to sleep before we had to get up to work cargo all the night tide. This went on, tide after tide, but the able seaman managed to get some rest between the tides and Father wasn't working cargo, so he got some sleep while we worked the cargo. As soon as the flood tide drove the carts away, we would have a meal of sorts, a wash and then bed. Father would get up when I went to bed and after about one hour would rouse me to come on deck and heave the vessel in further again, each time to get a bigger tide's work out. The able seaman refused to get up, but I saw the necessity, and couldn't refuse anyhow. We had four days and nights of this and I was about all in. We left there 4 a.m. on a Saturday and got to Falmouth about 8 o'clock. Father went ashore in another ship's boat and left us to clean up the mess on deck and scrub out our quarters for Sunday. I just felt completely worn out. For about twelve days I had not averaged two hours rest for a twenty-four hour day over the whole period and I simply had to stop. I went to my bunk without a wash telling the able seaman to do as he wished because I could do no more. The able seaman went to sleep in the galley and the first I knew was Father pulling me out of bed and telling me there was plenty of time to sleep over the week-end. I didn't answer. I was out on my legs. I remember feeling the tears coursing down my cheeks, and Father lifting me in his arms putting me back to bed. I went to sleep again and did not wake until Sunday mid-day. The able seaman told me afterwards Father would go below almost every hour to look at me and he was very worried. He said he didn't realise I was so worn out.

I quickly got over this episode and we loaded for Southampton, calling at Plymouth to pick Mother up and there we saw some yacht racing that gave Father a lot of pleasure. After leaving Plymouth we got above Start Point and as usual we were catching mackerel all the time and what we didn't cook we salted down for future use, which I didn't like, although to Father it was a cheap way of feeding the crew. We had quite a lot salted in and Mother knew I disliked salt mackerel and didn't want to catch any more. She suggested to me to put a salt one on the hook and tow it till Father came up, when he always made a bee line for the lines. Well at 8 a.m. the watch was called and of course the inevitable happened. When Father felt the line, he said, " There's a fish here," and as he pulled away, he saw it and at once started shouting at me for not attending to the lines properly as it wasn't struggling. Mother never turned a hair, until Father threw it in on deck and then she said, " Billie, you've caught a dead one," and she laughed and laughed till she cried, but not Father. I was in the watch alone and he turned on me in a fury. I saw it coming and was in the main rigging quick, with Father after me. I was too quick for him and was on the jump stay and across to the foremast before he got to the eyes of the main rigging with Mother nearly dying. He saw daylight too late and retreated looking rather foolish. It was all over soon, but Mother kept it up quite a time and the way he'd look at her would just make her go off again. No one but Mother ever dared make fun of him, but he took it from her because he had to, and I believe he was genuinely fond of her. . . .

It was about this time Father lost his elder sister, my Aunt Mary Ann Quance. The Slade family owed a lot to her and I myself felt her loss because she took more interest in me than anyone else in the family. If Uncle George made a model ship to sail, it always became mine, and there was no doubt I was the favourite with both Uncle and Aunt. As a boy I had spent far more time at their home than my own. Uncle George would draw a full rigged ship and name all the sails for my benefit. He taught me the compass and hundreds of other things about ships. I loved to listen to his sea yarns and hear of his voyages to China. Always good tempered, when my aunt would get a bit upset with him or irritated, he'd sing the old sea songs and his wife would call him an old blackbird and her irritation soon vanished. He never gave her an unkind word and, having no children, he must have missed her. The local Baptist minister persuaded him to take a Sunday School class. I'm afraid he didn't teach them much about the Bible. After reading a chapter he'd start the old sea yarns, greatly exaggerated no doubt, but the end of it was the boys wouldn't go to Sunday School unless Captain Quance taught them and, knowing how he could spin those yarns, I wasn't surprised. He had a hobby doing oil paintings and when he painted a certain ship, there was a wealth of detail and there was no mistaking who she was, because the shape of the ship and the cut of the sails would be perfect. One of his paintings, of our ketch the *Alpha*, is reproduced as an illustration to this book (Plate 6), but of course it loses a good deal by being in black and white.

Appledore up to this time had been a flourishing little seaport town. It was a fine sight to see forests of masts and sails going over the bar after Christmas. Sometimes up to 100 little vessels in one tide would leave the port. In calms a coil of ratline would be used to tow the ship. This would be made fast on the bowsprit end and the other end on the after thwart of the boat with a bowline. Two men would be in the boat with oars the length of the boat and according to the direction you wanted to pull the ship the bowline would slide from one side to the other, so that the boat would go from one bow of the ship to the other without easing on the oars. This would give the ship just enough movement to steer, but it was hard work especially when one of the boatmen was only a boy. The ship's boat was used for this purpose on craft up to 200 tons but in this case there would probably be four oars or sometimes three, all according to the number of crew carried and what was needed on board to work the ship.

All the sailors, with few exceptions, in those days joined the Royal Naval Reserve and as there was a training battery at Appledore it was the custom to do some drill between voyages. It was quite easy to arrange a few days' drill or a week, and get time off to look after the ships, especially those always trading to Bideford, Barnstaple or Fremington. This helped to keep these little ships going, as the R.N.R. money subsidised the low wages they could pay.

Many times as a youngster I have seen a crowd of sailors on Appledore Quay early in the morning, watching the bar and the weather. If they couldn't get over the bar, they would hastily put on their naval uniform and be off to the Battery at West Appledore. The men from Braunton would come from Crow and back in the evening, walking from the sandhills home. Those who manned the bigger ships going further away would arrange to spend Christmas at Appledore as they would nearly always have a month in which to do their drill. As they were paid wages by the trip (or voyage), the owners had to agree. In fact, some of the owners who sailed their own ships also belonged to the R.N.R. All the members of my family in the previous generation served 15 years first class. To entitle them to a gratuity of £50 they had to serve 20 years which nearly all of them would try to do. This £50 was a small fortune to some of them. The alternative was 5s. per week pension which helped the old age pension when that scheme came along. They also received a retaining fee every three months which I believe amounted to 21s. It can therefore be seen that when the Battery was discontinued, it was a severe blow to the seafaring classes at Appledore, both seamen as well as owners of the ships. This hastened the end of the small sailing vessels of Appledore, and fishing craft from Clovelly and Bideford suffered in the same way. It was indeed a blow at the whole merchant service as the men from Braunton, Barnstaple, Appledore and Clovelly were, I shall always believe, among the finest sailors in the world. They were famous for the way they handled small boats and in my opinion unequalled in the whole of the British Isles, both in rowing and sculling with a single oar over the stern, which most could do almost as soon as they could walk (Plate 7).

Then came the first world war. I was not at home at the time war was declared, but the R.N.R. was called up immediately, and I was told over 300 sailors left Appledore to report themselves for duty. Both masters and sailors left their ships lying in harbours all over the coasts and the owners of the ships couldn't find crews to man them. The result was a lot of old men and boys went to sea and kept them going for those four long years, but again the war was responsible for the ultimate ruin of the sailing vessel. True, they did well financially for the period of the war and a year or two after, but the men who manned them were gone. The fine seamen who had left Appledore wanted a different life. They had been promised " a home fit for heroes to live in " and they wanted their homes. Who can blame them? Some had died, some came back maimed. They had been all over the world in almost every naval action that was fought. . . .

Now the little ships are dead, some died naturally, some by enemy action, and like the men who manned them, they are only a memory.

CHAPTER 2

I BECOME MASTER

But to return to the subject of my own life, in which it can be seen I was rapidly becoming able to fulfil the role for which I was intended, we continued our trade between clay ports and Runcorn and Lydney or Newport to the Irish ports. One voyage we fell in with the *Maud Mary* (Plate 8) at Lydney. She was owned by my uncle and was about 140 tons, ketch rigged. The master's name was Ross. He must be nearing eighty now, but still in 1956 worked in an Appledore boat building yard. My cousin was eighteen, my own age, and he was mate. We left Lydney together, we were close together till we both arrived at Ballinacurra, we both loaded oats for Southampton and from Southampton we both loaded for Newport, Monmouthshire. During these three voyages we were further apart in harbour than we were at sea. The sailing qualities of both ships were so near equal, that we could have spoken to each other any day during the whole period. On the last trip we were becalmed just above Pendeen, short of food. One of the boats was manned by two hands from *Maud Mary* and as we were only three handed, as usual, one from our ship, which of course was myself. We pulled all the way to St. Ives, which was quite a few miles, bought our provisions and then pulled back again. We were just in time. We had only just delivered the goods and separated when a fine breeze came. The next evening we were in Newport. (For a more detailed account of this series of voyages in company with the *Maud Mary* see Appendix 2.)

One episode in my work while I was loading clay from barges at Teignmouth is worth recalling. We had used a chain sling for the cargo gin previously, but it was not available, being used for some other purpose. Now I had some iron wire strops in the store room, so I decided one of these might do for the gin on the gaff, but before putting it in place I took it to Father and asked him his opinion. He twisted and tried it every way and it certainly seemed all right, so with his consent I used it. The weight of a basket of clay was approximately two cwt. and the iron cargo gin about one quarter cwt. I was tipping the clay over the hatchway when just as I was handling the third basket, down came the gin, a drop of about forty feet. It struck my back a glancing blow and of course left me stretched out on deck. Mother was walking about aft and was soon on the spot. I couldn't get up on my legs, but I was helped aft and it was found I was bruised, etc., from the shoulder to the waist, nothing more serious than a week-end in bed. As it happened to be Saturday, Father worked in that barge of clay and I was fit again although rather stiff and sore on Monday morning. I didn't take much notice of it then, although I had been just six inches from certain death. I did, however, learn a lesson I've never forgotten. " Don't trust a wire strop that has been left about, unless the service has been taken off to look at it." That wire must have been gone under the service and Father must have broken it when he twisted it about.

After a few months had passed and we had put in some more voyages we got to Courtmacsherry and having discharged our cargo of coal, we loaded oats for Totnes in Dartmouth harbour. Now the weather was unsettled when we sailed and wind inclined to back southerly, so we kept away for Cork Harbour. After about half an hour Father decided to haul up to the wind again. It wasn't winter, and being about the end of July, we didn't expect to encounter very bad weather, but for me it was definitely uncomfortable as I felt more than usually seasick and indeed in all my life at sea I never completely conquered the habit, which was an annoyance as well as a great handicap sometimes.

The wind westerned again during the night and I was ordered (the usual performance) to go down and get out the chart and reckon up what the ship had done during the last eight or nine hours. " Give me a course and distance to the Seven Stones light-ship." This was done all right and after a time I began to feel better and was fairly well all that day and night. There was, however, a strong wind and we were just laying our course on the starboard tack. It came my watch on deck 8 a.m. on a Sunday. We had picked up the Seven Stones 'ship on the starboard bow and the sea was pretty bad. We had been unable to get any meat before we sailed, as there was no butcher at Courtmacsherry in those days, and our salt beef had all gone, so we came back on tinned beef. A tin of beef was opened and before relieving Father at the wheel, I was ordered to make a pie for dinner. We had our galley for cooking right aft in a specially built wheelhouse which was wheelhouse and galley combined. I had made the pie and was in the cabin clearing up the mess, when the ship went into an exceptionally heavy sea. She put her bow under, but worse still, when she lifted, her stern went down. Everything including the galley stove shifted and when I jumped up to see what was amiss, Father had put the becket on the wheel and was down in the scuppers, yelling at the top of his voice, " I shall lose my dinner," and he'd got the big boiler in one hand and was scooping pie dough and all together out of the water (which was rushing along the lee side) into the pot with his other hand.

This was too much for my already weak stomach, and instead of helping to retrieve his dinner, I was leaning over the lee bulwarks getting rid, most uncomfortably, of what I'd had for breakfast.

Father in his turn felt that was too much for him. He roared like a dozen foghorns calling me every kind of useless —— things in the world. I lost my temper, I think I was mad. I had had seven years as one of the crew and still sea sick, but the worst thing was to be told after seven years I wasn't worth thirty shillings a month. I was nineteen years of age and still useless in Father's eyes. Father was the first to recover himself He said, " Never mind what you heard me say. Forget it. You're all right," and a lot of other nice things I never heard before.

Well we weathered up the Runnelstone and arrived at Dartmouth too late to save our spring tide to Totnes. Father went home and while we lay there waiting for the next spring tide, we made our ship look like a yacht, masts scraped and varnished, rigging, which was hemp, tarred down, yards, booms and gaffs painted, bowsprit scraped and varnished, head gear painted white, bulwarks painted inside and out, and to finish the picture the decks were painted lead colour.

When the time arrived, we towed to Totnes and discharged our oats. I had a telegram from Father to proceed to Teignmouth under sail light. I knew it wasn't far, but I refused to go to sea two handed in a light schooner under sail and telegraphed back asking if I could engage the tug. Instead of a reply in the affirmative, Father came, furious. I met him on his arrival and I took it all. When he saw the vessel, his whole attitude of fault finding turned to a look of pleasure and I got the praise which I considered I deserved, but we had no tug. He sailed her to Teignmouth and went home again. We made that voyage to Runcorn and back to Falmouth and then loaded stone for Ilfracombe. We had a week-end home and then Father said, " I'm retiring this trip."

I answered, " Who is taking charge ? "

He looked at me, blazing again, and said, " Who do you think ? What have I been driving into you all these years. I'll make a man of you or I'll lose the lot."

I said, " *No*, Father, six weeks ago I wasn't worth thirty shillings a month, I can't get over that so quickly. I seem to have increased in value too quickly for my liking."

He said, " Don't flatter yourself. You aren't much good now, but you will be when I've finished with you. You can navigate the ship better than I can, but the best way to give you confidence and experience is to send you on your own." So in September, 1911, at the age of 19 I became master of a schooner.

I was far from happy but I little dreamt of the troubles I would have to endure until I finally kicked over the traces and became independent. My first voyage was from Lydney to Ballinacurra. On arrival in the river I was hailed from another schooner with bad news. My Uncle George Quance had gone out in his sailing boat, she had capsized in a squall and he was drowned, so I had lost both Uncle and Aunt who were most interested in me. I felt this pretty badly. They had both been good to me when I was young. He had lived to see me in charge of a schooner of which he was part owner, but he would never know how I ran the job or whether I was a success or failure.

We got up to Ballinacurra lower quay only to find all the berths occupied and at least a week to wait for a berth; and now the trouble started: for, of course, I wrote home and explained the delay and as it appeared to my father, I was to blame, as I ought to have been ahead of the others in making the passage across; but as they had left Waterford where they had been lying windbound, while I came straight across from the Bristol Channel, it was difficult to see how I was expected to travel three times further in the same amount of hours; but it was no use arguing with Father after his mind was made up. I only know when we

Plate 5.   *National Maritime Museum*

The boys of Appledore half a century ago, a group of W. J. Slade's youthful contemporaries, later to become the last generation of British coasting sailing ship masters and owners. They are, left to right:– Powe, Mike Powe, S. Peake, W. Blackmore (who was near his home, so he still had his boots and stockings on), J. Hammett, E. Yeo and J. H. Peake.

Plate 6.   *Original in the possession of Basil Greenhill*
A painting by George Quance of the ketch *Alpha*.

Plate 7. *National Maritime Museum*
Appledore boys could scull a boat like men at an early age. In the background are gravel barges waiting for the tide.

Plate 8. *National Maritime Museum*
The ketch *Maud Mary*, owned for many years by the Slades, the ketch *Thomas* coming up the Torridge under mainsail, and the small ketch *Trio* (not the Slade's *Trio* but another Appledore vessel) outward bound from Appledore.

did get a berth, we were half loaded with timber before our
inward cargo was finished and we got back to West Dock, Cardiff,
fairly quickly. We loaded for Falmouth and made a quick trip.

Now I was supposed to sail by the share, as all the others did.
I gave an account of the money and sent all the cash I could
spare to Father who was now the owner of all the ship. I got an
acknowledgment, but no comment on making a successful voyage.
I didn't write for a day or two, as we were waiting to go to the
Dean to load stone for Southampton and as this pier or loading
berth was in under the cliffs just to the westward of the Manacles
and wind southerly we couldn't load. Again this was all wrong.
I should write every day, giving the direction of the wind and
prospects. I solved this problem by writing twice every day till
we loaded and that was considered impudence.

However, we made another quick voyage, which eased the
tension somewhat and then took damaged cement to Newhaven.
When we left Southampton we went up through the Looe, a
passage inside the Owers bank. My uncles had purchased the
Lady of the Lake, a ketch, at Southampton and chartered her for
Newhaven as well, so we were in company, and my cousin in the
other ship was making his first trip as master. We got in first,
and it was very dark and blowing hard south west. The *Lady of
the Lake* got in shortly after, but a London barge coming behind
went ashore above the pier. I'm not certain whether she was
lost or if she was eventually salved.

My cousin loaded cement for Truro, I loaded whitening for
Glasgow. We sailed as soon as weather moderated after a fortnight
of south westerly gales, and got as far as Holyhead. We had one
night there and arrived at Glasgow two days after, having split
our foresail right across through the leechrope parting. I was
ordered by Father to put a stopper on it and over sew it, putting
a band across where it ripped. I put it ashore as I was working
cargo on the winch. It was repaired and fitted with a new
leechrope by a sailmaker for two pounds ten shillings. Again I
was wrong and wasting all the money, but I was learning to take
it as a matter of course and also learning to spend money, which
Father soon noticed when he didn't get as much as he expected.

In Glasgow I saw several skippers I knew and one was a friend
of Father's. These ships were Westcountrymen. There was the
iron ketch *Kindly Light* of Bude sailed by Capt. W. Fishwick of
Appledore, the *Mary Seymour* of Padstow, Capt. Walter Crocker

and the *Maria* of Fowey, Capt. R. Mitchell. They left Glasgow
before I did, but I was to get with them soon again. While we
were discharging in Kingston Dock, my mate started drinking.
He was notorious when in drink and I had heard once he started,
it was difficult to stop him. This time was no exception and it
gave me a lot of worry, so I made up my mind to get away from
Glasgow as soon as possible. Glasgow was a big port and suitable
sailors for schooners were scarce. Our crew consisted of mate,
able seaman, and a boy on his first voyage, whom I had shipped
at Newhaven. We shifted to the Terminus to load coal, so after
the No. 1 and No. 3 hatches were complete and we had made the
final shift to the main hatch, I went ashore to clear out and get
provisions for our voyage to Topsham. When I came back, there
was only the boy left. The others were ashore drinking and the
trimmers had left with the coal up under the foreboom. I was in
a pretty fix, so I got to work, finished trimming the cargo and
managed to get it all under the decks, and hatches battened down.
The crew came back drunk and went below where they remained,
while the boy and I shifted the ship off to the buoys.

I had ordered tugboat and pilot for 6 a.m. and although tired
out I slept little that night and was on deck 5 a.m. to find another
skipper of a nearby schooner, the *Emma and Esther*, trying to
persuade my crew to clear out and go with him. It appeared to
me I was being taken a mean advantage of by all concerned, but
he soon went after a bit of a row. We got the rope on the tug,
the mate was still below, and got down to Greenock where we
landed the Clyde pilot. The wind was easterly and I had visions
of getting back for Christmas, especially as the crew were rapidly
sobering up and we were under all sail. We were getting down to
Cumbraes, when the mate and able seaman appeared drunk
again. They had bottles of whisky stowed away which I knew
nothing about. To make matters worse the wind had shifted to
the south west and was freshening with black darkness. Being
well below Cumbraes I decided to try to get into Lamlash, but the
wind freshened and it became very dirty, so I put the topsail to
the mast and went aloft myself and took in the topgallantsail,
then down on deck and got the mainsail reefed. I felt very worried
with two men drunk and only the young boy, so then I thought
I'd go back to Rothesay. I never got the mate or able seaman
to come on deck at all as they were too drunk. While the ship
was hove to, I went below to have a look at the chart as I had

never been in Rothesay Bay. I satisfied myself there was nothing to worry about in going in there, so after getting the anchor and chain ready I squared away. I managed to get the topsail clewed up when we got well in to open up the Bay, and finally, got the head sails down, brought her up to the wind close in among the lights and let go the anchor. I went aloft and stowed the topsail and headsails and just put the gaff end gaskets on the fore and aft sails. It was about 3 a.m. when I finished and for the rest of the night I walked the deck in misery.

I had been through a trying seven years with Father but in all those years I hadn't been troubled with drunkards and I didn't know how to cope with them. After all I was little more than a boy in age. When daylight came, I felt happier and a little relieved to see the other three ships lying quite close to us and I knew I could turn to Capt. Fishwick for advice if the necessity came along. About 9 a.m. the mate got on deck with the able seaman attempting to get the boat out. The whisky had run out and they wanted more. I was determined to stop them and I stood up ready to enforce my order to leave the boat alone. Then a row started and in a short time Capt. Fishwick, who was watching us, was in his boat and came on board to back me up. The result was the mate gave in, our boat remained on board and no one but myself went ashore. Capt. Fishwick put his boat at my disposal during the whole fortnight we remained in Rothesay, and my crew were virtually prisoners. During those two weeks normal conditions were restored.

Eventually we sailed and during the voyage to Topsham the mate spent most of the time in his bunk with a bad head and I was glad when we arrived at Exmouth bight, where he was paid off. When we got up to Topsham, Father put in his appearance, unexpectedly. Mother was with him. It appears that Captain Fishwick had gone home from Totnes and met Father on Appledore Quay. The whole yarn came out and Father paid off everybody, leaving himself, Mother and myself to shift to Teignmouth where we got a fresh crew, or rather a mate and able seaman. When the ship was ready for sea, Mother and Father went home and we sailed for Runcorn where a coal strike held up shipping . . .

After discharging our cargo of clay, it certainly looked as if we were in for a long wait at Runcorn. Vessels had got loaded before the strike and were lying at Newferry windbound, and, having come along ahead of the next fleet, I was next on turn

if a cargo turned up, which did actually happen after a few days
waiting. We chartered to go to Northwich up the river Weaver
to load soda for Exeter. To get there I had to send the yards
down and strike both topmasts. The orders were to bring her to
sixty feet from the water line. When the topmasts were down
with the topmast rigging resting on the cap, I measured the height
of the trucks and found the measurement to the water line fifty
eight feet six inches which gave one foot six inches under the
guaranteed sixty feet which gave me a good margin. Imagine my
feeling therefore when we came to the first bridge to see both
topmasts touch the bridge about three inches from the truck and
break off in the sheave hole. In giving the measurement to me,
the authorities had forgotten to allow for heavy rains which had
swollen the canal waters.

This of course made them liable and the topmasts were paid
for without any argument or fuss. As a temporary measure I cut
fresh sheave holes in both the topmasts, refitted the bands for
topmast rigging and sent them aloft again. Leaving Weston Point
on the tug, after loading, we anchored at Newferry. We left again
the next morning under fore and afters and got to Redwharf Bay
where we anchored in a west south westerly gale with about five
or six other schooners. As soon as it moderated we left Redwharf
Bay, got below the Skerries and went away on the port tack, with
the wind blowing hard south west. All the others went to Holyhead,
windbound. The next day we were in sight of the Irish land when
the wind veered north west and I was obliged to heave to on
starboard tack. It blew very heavy, but we were fairly comfortable under double reefed mainsail and standing jib.

Now one of the vessels which went to Holyhead belonged to
Appledore and it appears the Holyhead-Dublin passenger boat
reported seeing a fore and aft schooner disappear in a squall off
the Kish, and that news soon got to my father's ears and it was
immediately assumed it was our ship. True enough, we had that
squall and I saw the passenger boat and during that squall I had
shortened down the sails to a minimum and perhaps we were
missed. It caused a lot of worry in my home and as we didn't
arrive at Exeter till about a week had passed, during which time
I had been in very bad weather, it was a relief when my arrival
was announced by telegram. I got a severe reprimand for staying
at sea, but I was too tired of fault finding to tolerate any further
letters of this description, so replied immediately that, as I was an

unsatisfactory master, I had decided to resign and go deep water.

This letter brought Father to Exeter by the first train, and when he came on board I was asked to explain what I meant, and of course I gave vent to my feelings in a way Father didn't expect. In the end I was persuaded to remain, and to help I was sent home to see Mother, so it all blew over. Father remained and I had a few days holiday. When I got home, Mother was upstairs and we came to the conclusion Mother ought to have some money, so I was very proud to give her five golden sovereigns. She said, " Is that all ? " so I doled out some more until it got to thirty and she still said, " Is that all ? " so I gave it up, but of course she was only putting on an act and I wasn't very quick on the up-take. Anyhow, I wasn't wanting money and was quite happy as long as I had enough for my needs, and I had no girl and no expensive tastes, so what was the good of money to me ? I had a lot to learn. . . .

After two more voyages we took a cargo for Bideford. After discharging, it was decided to go under carpenters at Appledore, so the crew were paid off. Then Father decided to rig the ship as a fore and aft schooner with squaresail yard aloft, which I didn't like as it was done only to save running costs, because we required a new lower topsail and other gear. So the fore yard was cut and made into a long fore topmast, the outriggers at the trestle trees were altered to go out straight as crosstrees, and a second hand gaff topsail made to fit. Altogether it was a successful rig and the schooner answered well, but we did miss our square canvas running in strong winds.

We loaded ball clay at Bideford for Glasgow and a crew was shipped consisting of the mate who was twenty-one, an able seaman of twenty-three, both belong home, and cook and ordinary seaman who hailed from London and was supposed to have a lot of rich relatives. The mate was a cousin and had already been mate of schooners for years out of Plymouth. He was certainly a very fine sailor and there wasn't much he didn't know about his job. We became firm friends and remained so until his death at the age of about sixty when he had been master in steam for many years. The able seaman was a carpenter of sorts and combined the two jobs as convenient to him. His failing was drink when he could get it, but never in the ship's hours, so I didn't have much trouble in that way. We were quite a happy family and we all worked well together.

We left Appledore in a fresh south west wind. Father came as far as the Braunton lighthouse with us, and then got into his boat after farewells, and away we went over the bar. As we opened out Hartland the wind freshened and we were obliged to take in the main gafftopsail and the flying jib and take two rolls in our mainsail We carried our fore gafftopsail to keep her quiet as there was a heavy beam sea. We had a proper washing going across the mouth of the Bristol Channel. The sea fell on board very heavy at times, but we picked up St. Ann's light Milford that night and eventually saw the South Bishop open out. There was no light on Skokholm at that time, but it wasn't difficult to navigate between the islands as long as the Bishops could be seen. As soon as we got to the Bishops we reefed our squaresail and got it on her and she didn't half travel up the St. George's Channel. That squaresail had to compensate for the loss of our square top-sails so we doubled the sheets and carried it longer than perhaps was wise. In any case we were discharging our cargo under a crane at the terminus, Glasgow, in less than sixty hours from the time we unmoored at Appledore. I found time to telegraph home and also phone our agent to arrange a charter to Ballinacurra. This had to be done between shunting trucks as we were working out the clay and I couldn't be spared for long. We shovelled out that 175 tons in a day and a half and loaded right away. I got a letter from Father before we sailed, congratulating me on making a very fast passage. Strange it may seem, but I hadn't thought of it until I got that letter and it was a red letter day, sure enough. Not only was I pleased, but Father was highly delighted which was something of a miracle.

At this time we were about to purchase a little double topsail schooner called the *Millom Castle*. I had written several letters to her owners before I left home and it had been arranged to survey her when she arrived at Cork where she was expected any day. I was told in the letter that she had arrived and Father was leaving home immediately. My orders were to hurry along as fast as possible, but we were the whole week getting there, and during that time, I was sailing along in Father's imagination faster than the previous voyage and he wanted to know where I had been wasting my time, which was quite a reversal of the last voyage. In any case I was in time to do the transfer, and the *Millom Castle* loaded oats for Padstow with Father as master. He left with a strong northerly wind, making a quick run, but she leaked like a basket. He wasn't unduly worried, because he knew she was a good little ship and to give Father his due, he was no fool in his knowledge of a schooner. It appears the owners had spent a small fortune on her, and she still leaked badly, for which reason we bought her at bargain price. There was another reason that contributed to our success in cutting the price and this was the loss of a number of shareholders. She was owned by William Postlethwaite and Sons of Millom in Cumberland and the owners of twelve sixty-fourths couldn't be traced. To end the deadlock another £150 was taken off the price and a guarantee was accepted from William Postlethwaite that he would be responsible for any claim arising in regard to the missing shares. We never heard any more about them up to the time we parted with the ship.

We left Ballinacurra for Cardiff with a cargo of timber and the *Millom Castle* went from Padstow to Newport in ballast. Father loaded for Courtmacsherry and I was pleased to find he had chartered me for Crosshaven. On the way down the Bristol Channel the *Millom Castle* was forced to go to the Mumbles, as she was leaking so badly that the pumps were continually in use. She was taken right in on Mumble flats and Father went searching for the leak which he found after an intensive search. He repaired it temporarily and eventually proceeded to Appledore, where a bad plank was cut out. After this she was one of the driest and strongest schooners on the coasts of the British Isles, and she paid us well through the twenty-five years we owned her. . . .

To return to our voyaging, we loaded scrap iron for Newport and then coal for Millbrook (Plymouth). When we were ready for sea the crew disappeared on the drink, so, as the mate had to go home for an operation, I decided to get down to Appledore. I telegraphed home to send a man to take her home " by the run." He arrived in the evening and we left. I never saw that crew for years afterwards when they admitted they wanted to spend Christmas at Newport, so tried to humbug me for a few days. Instead they were left stranded when their money was gone and I spent Christmas home. The mate went to the hospital immediately after Christmas and after a few weeks of bad weather we left home with Father and my brother on board. When we got to the Longships we had a strong southeast wind and it was a struggle to get up above the Manacles. Then we were heading well up and I could see we should be in Plymouth next morning, but Father came on deck and suggested going into Falmouth for the night. We disagreed over this and in the course of the argument I was told if I insisted on going on I would have to do it alone as Father was tired out and my brother sea sick. In the end I gave in, not without a growl, but I had my own back when I telegraphed to Mother from Falmouth as follows:—" Put into Falmouth, crew refused duty." I wrote a covering letter explaining the matter and Father got his leg pulled about that. We discharged our coal and loaded bulk manure for Bideford. . . .

After discharging that cargo we loaded timber for Garston, my mate had recovered and Father once more stayed home. Our voyage to Garston was uneventful but on our arrival we were greeted with the news that there was a dock strike on and we spent several weeks doing nothing. When the strike ended we soon got discharged and loaded for Bideford. In the meantime the *Millom Castle* had arrived home from London and it was found the vessel had been badly neglected and as several other unsatisfactory things came to light the master was discharged and Father went master of her himself. She loaded clay for Runcorn and arrived at Newferry in time to see us sail from Garston. Father pulled over across Liverpool River in the ship's boat to speak to me. My orders were to come to Runcorn immediately after arrival to take the *Millom Castle* for a few trips, whilst the *Elizabeth Jane* (my ship) was put in dry dock. In fact this was my last trip in my first schooner, much to my annoyance. I didn't like the idea of being put in a smaller ship and said so. If it was temporary I didn't mind, but when Father got tired of a ship he put someone else in her and I resented this. The excuse later on for leaving me in the *Millom Castle* was that I did so well in her during my first voyage that Father considered it better if I remained in her.

To return to my last voyage in the *Elizabeth Jane*. We got in over Bideford Bar on a Sunday evening and to Bideford. On Monday we started to discharge and I was off to Runcorn leaving Father to come home and square up the wages, etc., and also to collect my freight. On arrival to Runcorn in the evening I found the *Millom Castle* under the tip and Father all packed up ready to leave for home. I carried his bag to the railway station and that was the end of my day. As I had not received any of my freight at Bideford and had been at Garston a long time I was naturally short of money, so when we finished loading I went to the brokers to square up, thinking the inward freight had been left with the broker to pay Runcorn expenses. I was confronted with a bill for all discharging and loading charges and informed Father had drawn all the freight before he left and I was left with nothing at all, while Father had his own freight and mine, too.

This of course was grossly unfair as I was forced to draw on the outward freight the full third and pay interest at five per cent. to cover insurance, etc. I felt a bit upset about it, but I had got used to these things and once more started to work off the debts that were thrown on my shoulders. In this I was lucky as I made two or three quick voyages. The first was to St. Mawes, then with stone to Lymington where I undertook to land the cargo on the wharf for two shillings and sixpence per ton in addition to the freight. We did it all, from the hold work to winching it up, tipping in wheelbarrows, and wheeling it ashore. Then we shifted to Hamble to load loom for Cardiff where I met Father who had brought the *Elizabeth Jane* to Cardiff to load for Pentuan, Cornwall. I told Father about the unfairness in leaving me saddled with his debts and no money to pay them and of course, the usual happened and the matter had to drop. In any case I was now in funds and intended in future to remain that way. We carried on for some considerable time in the Irish trade and I found the *Millom Castle* a very handy little schooner as good as gold, tight as a drum and a good sailer, always among the fastest and as yet not very well known in the West Country. . . .

We continued our trade on the west coast and Ireland for the remainder of the year 1913, but perhaps the last trip before Christmas is worth recording. I was lying in Ballinacurra with another of our schooners called the *Doris* (Plate 9), owned by my uncle. Now the *Doris* was nearly loaded with oats for Poole in Dorset when we got in berth so, as the Captain had to go ashore to clear his ship outwards, I went on board to help finish stowing her cargo. This was a job where every care had to be taken, such as ramming the hatchway with hand spikes to make sure there were no empty pockets, etc. We had just finished when the master came back and the ship was unmoored at once. He insisted on me going down the river with him to see him out clear, which I did willingly, and when we said our farewells I wished him luck and, as a lovely fair wind was blowing, he was on top of the world. He said, " I'll be thinking of you here alone when I'm enjoying my Christmas home. I'll tell your Aunt Sarah all about

you," and somehow it jarred on me, so much that I started planning
to get a quick turn over. I went right back to an interview with
our coal merchant, who was also loading us with oats for Padstow,
and I suggested emptying our after hatch first, so that we could
load oats in that hold while we discharged out of the other hatch,
so that the horses brought oats to the ship and took coal out. I
kept them going by doing all the stowing of oats myself. In this
way we completed loading on the same day as we finished
discharging, sailing away in very quick time in a bid to get home
for Christmas.

On reaching the entrance of Cork Harbour we found a fresh
wind dead against us, which was far from promising, with only
four days to do the journey, but we plodded on feeling we might
get the wind north east as the North Channel opened up, so worked
well up to the eastward. On the third day we saw Trevose as the
darkness fell. At this time the wind went north north east and
freshened to such an extent that we had to double reef and heave
to, letting her drive steadily in towards Trevose. At dawn it was
one hour's flood and we were only three miles off the entrance
to Padstow when the main gaff broke. We got it down and fished
it, but were by this time close in, and as the tide had come on to
two and one half hours' flood I decided to run for Padstow, hit or
miss, and, being a stranger to the place, there was an element of
risk. Now I had heard Father talk of how he saved his life and his
ship when I was a baby, being caught off Padstow in a light ship
with a northerly gale and I had swallowed every word. It
appears he had to run for it just after low water. She went in
round Stepper Point, took the baffling winds, and he stuck her in
smooth water against the side of the Doom Bar. As the flood
came she dropped into deep water and he anchored in the cove,
riding out the gale. That night the wind died and backed
southerly and he left again. Arriving to Newport the following
day a report appeared that a sailing vessel, name unknown, had
grounded on the Doom Bar, and he kept his escapade quiet.

So much for the tale I had heard as a boy and now it was my
turn to run for the Doom Bar bearing in mind the baffling winds
around Stepper Point, we loosed the upper topsail and as we
bore away before the wind we set it, giving her plenty of speed.
As we got to the point where I expected to hit the baffling winds
we clewed up the lower topsail keeping the upper one on her
to the last second and as we hit these winds we let this run down.

A notice board in large print stuck up on the Stepper said, "Keep close to this point," which we did. We carried our headlong speed well into the cove, where we found the pilot was waiting. He jumped on board, came aft and said, "I know you're no stranger by the way you came in, but I suppose you'll take a pilot, Captain?" I laughed and of course answered in the affirmative and eventually after rounding Chapel Bar stuck on the ground between Padstow Piers. We moored, made arrangements for discharging and a new main gaff, then caught the last train through home for Christmas. On the evening of the 27th Aunt Sarah held a party, to which I was invited. We had just settled down when in walked the Captain of the *Doris* and his eyes bulged when he saw me. We greeted each other and I said, "I told Aunt Sarah you'd be coming along." It appears he had met strong east winds in the English Channel and had only arrived to Poole on Boxing Day, so I appeared to have had all the luck on this occasion. To my surprise Father didn't give a thought to the damage I had done on these two trips, he merely said, "I think you've done an excellent six months' work," and he was certainly pleased. . . .

In the New Year we got back to the Bristol Channel and Irish trade. We loaded for Castletownshend again and repeated a previous trip to Hayle with oats. While there I cycled to Redruth about ten miles away and renewed the acquaintance of my girl friend, whose father was in the ministry in that town. As soon as we met we were just boy and girl again. Soon after this I became engaged so saw quite a lot of Redruth and got to know a lot of people there belonging to the church.

We continued through the summer months, till July, in the Irish trade, and then as a change loaded at Cardiff for Charlestown, Cornwall. The freight for this was the lowest I'd ever received, two shillings and ninepence per ton, so we couldn't afford to lay windbound. I had been to Redruth on a few days' visit while the ship was discharging, and leaving there on a Friday I spent the night in a shelter on the promenade at Weston- uper-Mare, as I had missed the boat across to Cardiff. I didn't mind sleeping rough, being used to sleeping on a hard seat locker in the cabin when the weather was bad at sea. On this occasion I was rudely awakened by a police officer who asked me quite a lot of questions which I didn't appreciate at all. I didn't see I was doing any harm if I chose to have a night in the open air, but he was very suspicious of me and in answer to further questions

I was able to satisfy him that I was able, if I required, to book a room in the best hotel in the place.

I crossed over to Cardiff by the early boat on Saturday morning, did all the ship's business and sailed in the afternoon. Encountering a strong south west wind we just kept going till we got round the Longships. We arrived to Charlestown on Tuesday afternoon and after berthing, etc., I raced to catch the last train to Redruth. When I got to the Manse there was no one at home, so I sat down to weigh things in my mind. The trouble was I was not very presentable. In the rush to catch the train I hadn't put a collar on and I hadn't shaved for four days, and now I was outside the Manse, stranded. Well my first guess was right, I called at a certain house and there at a party was the one I wanted. I was pulled inside whiskers and all before I realised what was on. I was given a good welcome and spent an enjoyable evening even though I had not slept in a bed for a week. That night I slept like a log, waking the following morning at six o'clock. I was out in the garden enjoying the fresh air before the family awoke and that day I took my future wife back to Charlestown with me. I wasn't long doing my business and chartering for London. After a few hours at Truro we returned to Redruth by the last train.

CHAPTER 3

THE FIRST WORLD WAR

WE WERE ABOUT four or five days in Charlestown and left there catching a fine north west wind up channel to London. We chartered there with cement for Minehead in Somerset and while waiting for orders off Swanscombe I had the news that we were at war with Germany. I happened to have an Irish crew and a Danish mate. The Irishmen got some drink in their stomachs one day and they went to war with England too, and me in particular. During this happy evening they were going to fight for " home rule " and drive all Englishmen to blazes. I took no notice, just went below out of sight. I survived all the threats to my person and the next day it had all blown over as I thought. We loaded and sailed, having a fairly quick passage, arriving to Minehead in the evening. The vessel was barely moored before my Irish crew started kicking up again, demanding their wages as they were leaving at once. I tried to reason with them, telling them I hadn't sufficient cash to settle up till next morning, but it was useless. The mate went below and locked himself in his stateroom, and these two men just set about me and I had to defend myself for the first time since I was a boy. Well, being quick, strong, and in splendid health, I got the better of the argument against the odds. They cleared out ashore and reported me to the Customs, where I was invited to explain why I had struck these men. I explained the position and invited the mate to tell what he knew and in the end the Irish in them came out again, and after more dire threats the officer had all the evidence he needed to know how to act. I got rid of them at once, borrowing sufficient money from the harbour master, Captain Perkins, who was well known to me when he was master of the famous local schooner *Periton*.

These two men were prosecuted for attacking the master of a brigantine they were in shortly after and both went to prison, so I was lucky again.

I went home and found Appledore deserted. All the sailors had gone to the Navy and Father had several ships left in different ports with no crews. He himself had gone to Llanelly to fetch one, and he got two old men to go to Holyhead to another, while the third one was in Falmouth with only the captain left on board. We were all disorganised for a few weeks, but we got along somehow. I got a man with a crippled foot to come with me and he proved a splendid shipmate. I was indeed sorry when he left me about eighteen months later.

We made a few voyages to Ireland and back to the Bristol Channel, with just three men all told and were quite happy and comfortable. On one of these voyages we came back to Lydney in ballast and being a fair wind we threw the ballast overboard on our way up the Bristol Channel. The weather was thundery and freshened to the northward, blowing hard. We reefed down and my mate, the Dane, was nervous of carrying sail on an empty ship, but she was very handy. We beat up through the Shutes in the River Severn. After passing the Lloyd lighthouse a heavy squall was brewing in over Chepstow, I got her in to the weather shore head to the eastward when it struck us solidly and over she went on her bulwarks with the topsail sheets flying. She just went broadside on, flat on her side, up over everything. By the time we got close up to Lydney Pier it eased and she came up on her bottom in command again. I then did the only possible thing, steering for the mud bank just below the pier, she took the ground on her fore foot, her stern in deep water swung round, we let the sails run, dropped the anchor on the ground to steady her as she floated off and dropped alongside the pier in the entrance to the basin and as the lock gates opened we had plenty of help to heave her in the basin.

I must say here in those days a lot of sailing vessels from Appledore, Bridgwater, Braunton, Gloucester and other Bristol Channel ports traded to Lydney and it was the practice when necessary to join in helping each other. In busy times the sailors and lockgate men would all join in working together and a happier fraternity never existed in the British Isles. It was a very rare occurrence to see anyone having hard words, in fact, one felt at home with everyone when entering Lydney docks. Lydney was not only comfortable and easy, but the cheapest port in the channel. The harbour dues on a one hundred and eighty tons D.W. schooner would be under ten shillings and the trimming of the cargo about fourpence a ton, the shipper paying twopence per ton to the captain on all house coal as gratuity. All these ships sailed the Severn without pilots. . . .

It was all St. George's Channel trade and clay ports for the next few months, but in the end I was back again to the Bristol Channel and Irish trade. One thing that happened during my trips to Ireland shocked the world. I left Kinsale for Lydney on the same day the *Lusitania* was sunk. Up to this time we had carried on our work and hadn't worried about submarines, but the time was at hand when we had to watch our step.

It was certainly getting dangerous and I wanted to work my way round to Falmouth as I intended to be married at the first opportunity. To this end we loaded coal for Falmouth. We got as far as Appledore with weather rather unsettled and Father was home again, having found a crew for his ship including a new master. Several vessels were at Appledore all bound to the Falmouth district. When we sailed there were quite a little fleet competing for the lead. The wind was about west north west and we had to beat over the bar, and most of them got a good bit ahead of us working short tacks. We were the only schooner and of course the ketches were handled easier and quicker till we got out clear of the bar. One of our ships, the ketch *Progress* took the lead and we never caught her. My cousin was master of her and she got well down in the Bay before we cleared.

The first casualty was the *Ulelia*. She went ashore on Airy Point in a dangerous position and as Father was her owner, he went out to her. They got her off again that night, but she missed her passage. The others were the well-known ketch *Hobah*, the *Julia* and our ketch the *Lady of the Lake*, and several others bound for Boscastle and Padstow.

The *Progress* got far enough down to save the ebb round Hartland, which put her a considerable distance ahead, as she was able to cheat the tide below Hartland. The rest of us got jammed in the race and drifted back on the flood. That night the wind backed southerly and freshened to a strong wind. We were first round Hartland on the tide and we carried a heavy press of sail all that night on the port tack. The next morning we only saw one ketch astern but Pendeen was about three points on our port bow and we were a long way off the land, we had to reduce sail and tack ship. At dark that night we were just above Pendeen and close in. It was now blowing very hard south. We put three rolls in our mainsail and reefed our topsail. The ship was now rigged as a " Garibaldi schooner " with only one big topsail with a reef in it and one yard, less weight aloft for going without ballast. We found it pretty tough when we opened out Mount's bay and we did our best to get up above the Runnelstone, which we just failed to do before the tide again drove us back. Again the *Progress* being further ahead just managed it, although I didn't see her till we arrived to Falmouth next day, when we compared notes. It was a hard struggle and we were about six hours behind the *Progress*. We were the only ones who got round. The others went to St. Ives Bay and both *Progress* and ourselves loaded stone for clay ports and went up along together before the rest arrived. We were for Charlestown, *Progress* was for Par.

We loaded at Charlestown for Runcorn and during our stay at Charlestown I got married. After a week-end away I brought my wife to Redruth and went back to my ship, leaving almost immediately. We made several trips to Runcorn and back to the English Channel, the last one to Plymouth, and as it was getting close to Christmas we loaded manure for Newport, Monmouth-shire, then to Fowey where my crew left the ship to go home for Christmas. This is where I started to come up against trouble, as it seemed impossible to replace a crew once you lost them and in this case the able seaman was discontented because he was away from home too long and he persuaded the mate to go with him. I managed to get Christmas with my wife, leaving the ship under the care of Fowey pilots. When it was over, my wife joined me on board for a week, we chartered for Preston and I had a boy from Appledore. We loaded and it was hard work to clean up and batten down practically alone. There wasn't a sailor anywhere and I was almost in despair when a telegram came from Father that a mate was on the way. When he arrived, I almost groaned. He had always acted as cook previous to this, and wasn't big enough to look over the rail. It was just another boy. However, the wind went north west and we sailed, getting to Falmouth that night.

I tried hard to get a man during the next few days, but eventually left, hoping for the best. We got round the Longships and squared away for the Smalls with a strong westerly wind.

Plate 9.   *H. Oliver Hill*
The topsail schooner *Doris* built at Salcombe and owned by the Slade family
from 1910 until her loss on the French coast in 1918.

At Appledore boys and girls became intimately familiar with boats as soon as they could walk.

I had two rolls in the mainsail and we were doing well. Now I hadn't left the wheel for about twenty-four hours and I was feeling tired so asked the mate if he could steer her. " Oh yes," he replied. I was rather worried as he looked so small behind the wheel and hadn't the strength to do it for long. I stood beside him for a while and he seemed to manage, so I said I'll go below and rest my feet for a little while. I'd just got my sea boots off when she gave a heavy lurch and a nasty sea fell on board. When I jumped up he was yelling at the top of his voice. He'd let her broach and got frightened, so I took her again and never left it till I anchored at Holyhead worn completely right out.

The next few months were the hardest of my life. There was no sleep or rest at sea and I often had my eyes bloodshot and painful on arrival in harbour. At Holyhead I met the *Elizabeth Jane*, my first command. She was sailed by an Appledore man and Father had sold him a quarter of her, as he was a real good man. He had left Par for Runcorn while I was held up for a crew and was now lying windbound with flour for Penryn. He came on board and I suppose it was natural he should be rather cock-a-hoop at being so far ahead of us; he pulled my leg in a good tempered way and when we sailed next day came on board to help us out, and being only half manned I was grateful. We got to Preston although the weather remained bad, and, after discharging, we also loaded coal for Penryn. In an attempt to catch up with *Elizabeth Jane* we sailed in a strong southerly wind and that night off the Skerries the wind veered and blew hard northerly and finally north east. When I got to Penryn we were the first arrival. It appears the fleet were all jammed in together at Holyhead and when the wind veered it blew too hard for them to get out. I had the last laugh again and I went home that night very tired but very happy.

Towards the end of the summer of 1916 I had a letter from Father saying he had purchased a little schooner called the *Gleaner*, built at Carrickfergus. She was about one hundred and eighty five tons D.W. and I was requested to get a master for the *Millom Castle* so that I could go to Dublin to take charge of her. I got a master for the *Millom Castle* all right, but when we arrived to Preston I found Father had messed things up through not paying a deposit and the *Gleaner* was sold to Falmouth for more money. As the new master of the *Millom Castle* had left another ship to take mine I was in a mess too, as I couldn't back out of my agreement

with him even if it was only a verbal one, so I packed my bag and
went home. My brother who was sailing with me also had to go
home as the new master had his crew arranged. This thoroughly
upset everybody.

In the meantime Father had to go to sea again for a few trips
in the ketch *Trio* (Plate 11). He loaded for Ballinacurra and on
his arrival he went to Cork on business, saw a fine schooner arrive
called *W. D. Potts*, and immediately agreed to purchase her, so
I was off to Cork, bag and baggage, to do my part in the business
and take charge of her.

She was really a fine ship carrying about one hundred and ninety
tons built at Pwllheli, near Portmadoc. I already held substantial
shares in the *Millom Castle* and it was agreed I should have sixteen
sixty-fourths of the new purchase. After taking over from the master,
who was also owner, I noticed a rat trap in the store room. I asked
the late owner if there were rats on board. He assured me there
were not, but he always kept a trap in case one should come on
board. This was a deliberate lie, as I soon found out that night. I
went to bed and woke up at a noise in the cabin, and when I looked
out in the dim light there were four or five rats on the cabin table.
I spent the rest of the night throwing boots, etc., at them when
they came out. It was my first experience with these vermin and
I was determined to get rid of them, so I had her fumigated which
made them quiet for three months, when they came back as
numerous as ever, but in the end I cleared them all with back
break traps. I would buy all sorts of bait and when setting the
traps would handle them with my gloves on and smoke them
always before and after catching a rat. I have sat in the cabin
with a trap in each cupboard and caught a dozen in one evening,
which will give some idea of how numerous they were.

Now, after we had settled in I chartered with timber for Garston,
and as the mate, an Irishman, had left with the late captain,
Father sent his mate from Ballinacurra to join me. This young
man was only nineteen and had been brought up with his father
in a ketch trading mostly from the Bristol Channel to Barnstaple
and Bideford. He had never been in a schooner, but nevertheless
he was a good sailor and could be trusted on deck in all weathers.
He was also my cousin and I was determined to push him on.
The rest of the crew were two Norwegians and a boy of fourteen
as cook. We seemed to be well manned, which was something I
had not had for a long time and I felt rather elated at the prospects.

Alas, I was soon undeceived, we finished loading and the wind being north west I told the mate to get the topsails loosed as I intended leaving, but before doing so I ran to the post office sending a telegram to our insurance to cover the ship from that day. When I came back, the topsails were loose, but the crew had gone, leaving me with the mate, who, as stated, was a novice in schooners, and the boy. This didn't stop us. We cast off our ropes and with topsails set were off down the river.

To make matters worse the boy injured his hand in getting up the mainsail and was a passenger from then on. When we got to Queenstown I was afraid to anchor as the ship had very heavy anchors and cables and I thought if I let go anchor it'll never get up again, so after discussing the position with my cousin we agreed to carry on and try to make the voyage. We had it fine till we got above the Tusker, then wind backed southerly and began to freshen. We put a reef in the mainsail and I went aloft to stow the upper topsail; being used to the job it was no trouble. I determined to go to Holyhead if I could make it. When it came dark on the second night out we picked up the South Stack, but we were not destined to enter the harbour. The mainsail, peak and main halyards were of chain on small winches and I didn't like the look of it when I saw it, and my distrust was justified, for as we were passing the North Stack the peak halyards parted and down came the gaff end, this caused the jaw rope to part and the gaff came away from the mast, the main halyards jammed and it was impossible to make Holyhead in this condition, so I kept away outside the Skerries to get room to move. My cousin and I got aloft and after hard work got the sail down. We got some blocks and fitted for peak halyards and being short of rope used a three inch coir winch line. We were well up above Lynus before we got the mainsail set again. Then the head of the staysail went and we had to haul it down and repair it temporarily. We got that set again and the boom jib bursted.

I began to wonder if the ship was fit to be at sea at all as our gear seemed to be all rotten and unfit to stand up to any strong weather. When daylight came the wind had gone more to the westward and I made up my mind to run for Liverpool Bar. We got our anchors and chains ready while both of us could help in the job and then squared away. We got to the bar and all was going well till we got to the Crosby Channel where the patrol boat was stationed. He approached and fired an order at us,

" Let go your anchor." Well any sailing ship man would know
you can't let go anchor until sail had been taken in, so we did
our best to shorten down, but the fool in charge of that patrol
boat never gave us a minute to handle the ship. He barked out,
" Let go your anchor immediately or I'll fire at you." We got
the topsail clewed up and I put the helm down and rushed forward
hauling down jibs and with everything flying away we were forced
to anchor all standing. That man was the biggest idiot I ever
came across during the first world war. It took forty-five fathoms
of chain to bring her up and when we did manage it she was
going hausepipes in every jump. The sea was pretty heavy as the
Crosby bank was not ebbed dry. It went smoother after a few
hours and now my dread was to heave in all the chain and the
heavy anchor. They kept us there till dark and then ordered us
to heave up and get our towrope ready. We hove away, but it
was an endless job running from the wheel to the windlass, but at
last it was done and we were towed to New Brighton where we
again anchored with each of us exhausted. Why that man made
us anchor and gave us all that work, with his utter lack of
common sense I never knew, but I do know we might have lost
that ship through being forced to carry out the orders of a man
who was unfit to do his job. I traded to the Mersey continually
for some months, but was never served like this again, so perhaps
someone with more knowledge of the handling of sailing ships
was put in charge.

I got ashore the next day and arranged for a tug to come
alongside to help get the anchor and tow us to Garston and I
felt relieved to be in dock, safe. We spent several days at this
port repairing sails and reeving new gear, condemned all the
mainsail chains and put rope, so when we left we were certainly
better equipped with running gear, although some of our sails
wanted to be renewed. After a few trips we had new boom jib,
standing jib, staysail and lower topsail. As the mainsail was
fairly new we were well found.

On one of these trips we had left Falmouth with a ship
belonging home and we were badly beaten because she was a
faster ship altogether than ours. When we got to Cardigan Bay
the wind came down north east and blew hard. As usual our
sails started to go and I had to run back for repairs. That made
me insist on new sails and when I arrived to the Mersey the other
ship was ready to leave. We got the new sails on her and were

ready to leave again. I was surprised to see my friend still lying at Newferry as we passed down but we carried on to New Brighton. It was blowing hard right up the river and I had a very narrow escape of running into Liverpool Landing Stage. We reached in close to it and I gave the order to tack when the wheel suddenly became useless. I realised in an instant that something was wrong with the wheel chains. I opened the wheelhouse door and saw everything adrift. I got hold of the iron tiller on the back of the rudder head and pulled for all I was worth. She came round only just in time. I kept the topsail aback while we hurriedly repaired the chains and we reached New Brighton safely where we remained for the night.

It was blowing very hard north north west next morning, but we left under single reefs and we had plenty water coming on board till we finally cleared the bar, when we set sail and drove her hard for the Skerries, which we rounded in quick time. I had purchased a light balloon staysail and after weathering the Skerries we set the squaresail braced well forward with the weather tack on the cat head. The balloon staysail was set on the boom jib stay and she raced along with everything drawing faster than I'd ever seen her travel. We had plenty of good gear and I wasn't afraid to drive her. When we sighted Pendeen it was blowing so hard that I was afraid I'd lose the balloon staysail if I tried to take it in, but the wind was steady, so I decided she could drag it till dark when I could run off before the wind and take it in. We rounded the Longships before dark and the previous two hours she had repeatedly put the foam through the hausepipe. We double reefed the mainsail to run up the English Channel, the wind steadily freshening, and at dawn we were in Falmouth. When we got back to the Mersey on the next voyage, most of the schooners we had left at Newferry were still there, so I had done very well. The next voyage back to Penryn was our last that year as we laid up for Christmas.

It was February, 1917, when we loaded our next cargo, which meant a long voyage, but freights were good and the holiday did us good too. We had an uneventful trip to the Mersey and back to Flushing, then loaded for Glasgow which proved to be the last voyage for the *W. D. Potts*. I had got to admire my little ship. She was really good for going to sea and standing up to bad weather. She was also as tight as a drum in all weathers. I had also done a lot of alterations to sails and rigging.

E

I could set more canvas and by altering the out-riggers of the fore topmast backstays I was able to brace the yards up better to lay one point closer to the wind. On her last trip we beat up to Lundy, the wind north east, following the government route among about a dozen ships, some of whom were considered fast, and to my surprise and pleasure we were as good as the best of them, which shows how our sailing had improved.

We had a fine passage and one night while becalmed off the Isle of Man we drifted past what I took to be a floating mine. It was a good moonlight and this object was only a few feet away. It had horns sticking from it and I was glad to see it drift away clear. The next evening we were about ten miles off from the Wigtownshire coast, in company with a big full rigged ship, when a German submarine surfaced about one hundred yards away and immediately opened fire on us without warning. We rushed to get out our boat and although it generally took two of us to lift her stern with the after tackle, in this instance, I did it alone while the rest of the crew pulled up the bow. She was just clear of the rail when all the yards and mast head came tumbling down and although we all got away unhurt a hole was knocked in the boat, and I kept bailing water until we landed at Portpatrick in the early hours of the next morning. It was a rather hectic time while it lasted and we have nothing to say in favour of our German enemies who kept firing regardless of our situation until our ship disappeared and only the quick and competent way in which our crew worked in getting the boat in the water saved our lives. It was in keeping with the Kaiser's policy of sink at sight. The ship in our company was also sunk by gunfire. She was in ballast and as she settled down she fell over on her yards at first and just before the final plunge suddenly righted herself and then disappeared with a lot of debris flying in the air. That was a sight I shall never forget.

After approximately six hours we landed, about 2 a.m., and were challenged by a sentry guarding the approach to the wireless station. After satisfying the sentry, we were escorted to the house of the officer in charge, who treated us splendidly, and when he heard my name he wanted to know my birthplace, and strange to relate he knew my grandfather very well and was most interested to meet me. . . .

After a week home I was informed I had to get another ship or join up in the services, so I went to Appledore to see my father about the future. He of course was upset at the loss of a fine ship, but after our talk it was decided I should join my brother in our ketch *Trio* as mate till we could buy another ship, but in the meantime prices soared and we found ourselves unable to do this. The *Trio* at that time was only doing short trips in the Bristol Channel and my brother wasn't experienced enough to go further than that, but as soon as I joined her I found her chartered for Preston. We did about six months of this trade and of course I was master at sea and mate in harbour with no extra wages. This was no fault of my brother's as he continually requested me to ask Father to put us on an equal footing. My brother was a single man and all the money went home. However, I eventually purchased sixteen sixty-fourths and I then insisted on equality. I found the *Trio* was by no means slow, in fact she was among the fastest by the wind. We fell in with the famous *Katie Cluett* leaving Holyhead one voyage and when we were both weathering down Bardsey on the starboard tack under single reefs there wasn't a quarter of a mile between us. Among a fleet of five or six schooners, we were the only ketch and we all drove as hard as we could to make Fishguard. When we got to Fishguard only one ship was anchored there and she proved to be the very famous and fast *Rhoda Mary*. Our time of arrival was 9 p.m. The *Katie Cluett* came in 11 p.m. and the others did not get there till the next morning This should be proof that the *Trio* could hold her own among the best. (For a more detailed account of this race with the *Rhoda Mary* and the *Katie Cluett*, which were considered by many people to be the fastest of all the merchant schooners, see Appendix 2.)

I remember one trip leaving Charlestown for Preston with the *Emily Millington*. She was some distance ahead of us at the Lizard and her captain, a friend of mine, was very fond of leg pulling. He certainly felt his ship was a wonderful little schooner, as indeed she was, and in his estimation much too good for the *Trio*. Well, after getting round the Longships we carried away our topmast, and, as there was a nasty sea, I couldn't do anything about it till we got across to the Welsh coast. Then we set to and got down the stump, which was fairly long, as it had gone in the cap, cut a fresh fid hole, and sent it up again. Then I cut the upper part of the weather of the sail to fit a yard on it, so that when set the upper end of the yard was above the truck. It was in fact a jackyard topsail and set in its place perfectly, in fact during the time I was in her it was never altered. Of course I had lost sight of the *Emily Millington* by this time but we got above the Bishops blowing fresh south west and dirty. We got to Preston and my friend wasn't there. He arrived when I was leaving, coming alongside to speak to me. It was of course my turn to do the leg pulling, but of course I was lucky. . . .

When Christmas drew near we were at Falmouth loaded for St. Malo and I was anxiously hoping to catch a convoy quickly in order to get back for the holidays. We sailed about one week before Christmas and being a stranger to the place I acquired a good sheet in case I should have to enter without a pilot. As it turned out this was fortunate for me. We were close in the Cape Frehel with wind south west about midnight when it suddenly veered northerly and blew a gale. We were on a leeshore and I was driving her off when I found she was leaking badly and we couldn't leave the pumps. At dawn the situation was desperate, so we decided to run her for St. Malo, hit or miss. Eventually we anchored in the roads and it took all hands four hours to get her pumped dry. Utterly worn out, we slept the rest of the day and in the evening got under way and sailed in the docks, strange to say she had become tight in smooth water and it was some time afterwards we discovered she would open the blind seam in bad weather, which caused her to leak like a basket. This was cured by fitting iron bilge stringers which effectually tied her up.

There were several schooners (British) lying there and we were not in turn for discharging. We moored close to one and when the men, including German prisoners, came to discharge her all hands were ashore including the master—on the drink. They asked if we were ready and I answered in the affirmative so we started and the next day we finished and ordered our ballast. The third day we were ready for sea and the cry went round among the crowd that I must have bribed my way through, but I never even thought of it. I was just plain lucky, and of course quite sober.

We sailed and got back the English side fairly quick. On the night before Christmas Eve I was running down for Falmouth. It was blowing hard east south east and I knew if I ran down to the opening of the boom defence in the heavy sea being light she would never beat back to Falmouth entrance again, so determined to jump the boom defence, hoping I should not be seen by the authorities. We blacked out our lights very carefully and I never

felt her touch the wires. As soon as I was in a favourable position
I took the canvas off from the side lamps and then saw the patrol
boat who gave us the all clear, but I wonder what would have
happened had they known I had come in over the boom defences.
I expect I'd have been shot.

During one of these trips in the *Trio* a little episode took place
which may be worth recording. As far as I can remember it was
in March, 1918. We had got above Pendeen, running along with
a fine breeze and rather dirty weather keeping rather further off
than usual in those hazardous times because I was afraid the wind
might veer north west. I was on deck alone, just coming dawn,
when I heard voices shouting, " Pick us up, don't leave us." This
startled me and looking to leeward I saw some men in the water
clinging to the wreckage of a lifeboat. I yelled out, " Jump up ! ",
to my crew and at the same time put the helm down, letting our
big staysail, which was rigged out as a spinnaker, run across the
mast all aback, which effectually deadened the speed to practically
nil. By the time the crew came on deck I had the gripes off the
boat ready, and over the lee rail she went quick.

Up to then I hadn't thought of who was going in her. We
were only three all told and the boat was only fourteen feet, not
very big for picking up a crowd of men in a sea way. It was decided
for me in a few seconds by my brother. I said, " All right, you two
look after the ship, I'll go." I had to scull with a single oar over
the stern about 200 yards and it never occurred to me till I got half
way that I was a non-swimmer, and this thought set my brain
going, as I knew there was little chance if I capsized or filled my
boat, with no air tanks in her. However, to handle a boat comes
natural to an Appledore bred person and any of my fellow
townsmen would have done what I was trying to do. The risk
was really small if those men were reasonable. When I got within
twenty feet of her I saw the wrecked lifeboat was going up and down
in the sea, sometimes submerged altogether, and it struck me to go
alongside in the orthodox way might not only catch my boat
under the bilge and capsize her, but the men might panic and all
grip one gunwale together which was bound to upset us.

The solution to this difficulty came instantly. Our boat had a
very round stem and iron stem band. I would scull stem on so
that my boat's stem would slide down over the wreckage and try
to pull one at a time in the boat. I selected the youngest who
seemed pretty lively and got him in over the bow. I said " Pull

the others in while I keep the boat end on." This he did and I
was soon sculling back with our five living and one who collapsed
and died in the boat, six of us all told. I got alongside on the
leeward side again and I talked to the young seaman who understood English, explaining exactly what had to be done, and any
failure on his part would put us all in the water. He certainly
came up to scratch. The tackles, which hung from the mast (no
davits) were hanging over the side and at the first roll of the ship
towards us I shouted, " Hook on," and the sailor did so. With
my brother on one tackle and our able seaman on the other they
simply gathered in the slack and as our ship righted herself after
the roll the boat was on the rail. We got out on deck and lifted
out the unfortunate man and then lowered the boat on deck.
The young man speaking English told me he was mate of a
steamer torpedoed in the early hours of the morning, and I had
indeed heard a heavy explosion several hours before. The
torpedoed ship's name was the *Skrymer* of Christiania, I think
I've spelt the name correctly. I gave some dry clothes to the men
and a hot drink and food, which soon cheered them up by a warm
cabin fire. We made for St. Ives bay as quick as the wind would
take us, and only about an hour after we picked them up we were
signalling for a boat about 100 yards or so from the pier. The
boat came quickly and when we parted the mate shook hands and
with his voice full of emotion said, " THANK YOU, but for you
we should have lost our lives."

During the summer we made several trips from the Bristol
Channel and the Mersey to Coverack. This suited my brother
as he was engaged to marry a very nice girl who lived there, but
I soon tired of that and chartered for Isigny, a small port close to
Carantan where our army landed on D-Day so many years later.
It was an awful worry to me when our army landed as I knew the
coast so well and it was a lee shore, I really couldn't understand
how they could do it. I walked Bideford Quay thinking about the
loss of life. I was on the Quay till 2 or 3 a.m. watching the weather
and praying for the wind to die away. I didn't know about the
Mulberry harbours of course and I was full of admiration when I
did find out.

We made our voyage to Isigny and when we got back I made
up my mind to have a change of ships. My brother was now
capable of running the *Trio* on his own and I left her at Falmouth.
I wrote to Captain Fishley and recommended the master of the

Millom Castle to them as they were running a fleet of schooners, and I was glad to learn he was appointed master of the schooner *Dispatch*. This left the way open for me to join the *Millom Castle* due back at Cardiff from Morlaix in France. When she arrived I went there and found the captain in bed with influenza, and when he recovered and went home I got an attack myself, although mild, from which I soon recovered. The ship had hit something and we feared damage to her bilge, so after she was empty we hove her down on her side in the West Dock to examine her. This wasn't very difficult and the carpenters were able to do the repairs in the ship's boat, as the bilges came well out of the water when hove down. We chartered for St. Vaast La Hogue, again back to the area I had just left. We got to Falmouth quick, just as the Armistice was signed. . . .

CHAPTER 4

THE COMING OF THE MOTORS

THE YEAR 1919 opened with great promise, the war was behind us, but we still retained our guns. I was now settled down in the *Millom Castle* and after the order came to remove the guns it seemed that normal trading would soon be on the way and I felt happy. About this time my brother left Bideford Grammar School. My father had arranged to apprentice him to one of the big London shipping firms, intending him for the deep water trade, but George had other ideas and insisted on joining me in the *Millom Castle* as ordinary seaman, so to Fowey he came and soon settled down to a life in coastal schooners. I must confess I was pleased to have him with me, as it was awfully difficult to get crews at this time, and what we got often caused people like myself, who didn't indulge in intoxicating liquor, a lot of worry.

Despite its opening promise the whole of 1919 was a nightmare, I could do nothing right no matter how hard I tried.

Several Braunton ships now had motors fitted and my cousin also had an auxiliary motor fitted in the ketch *Progress*. I made up my mind to approach my father to get him to agree to having an auxiliary motor installed in my ship in order to compete with others. It seemed to me I was getting nowhere up to then and I was discontented. My father agreed on condition that I would shift my home from St. Austell to Bideford. An engine was ordered from Messrs. Widdop and it was arranged to have everything ready so that a quick job could be done.

I made up my mind to keep going till it was all ready. I chartered for Penryn, made a quick trip and on arrival got the news that everything was ready for the installation. We got a cargo of stone for home and the work started. It was soon discovered there was a part missing, so, instead of three weeks, it was three months before we completed the job. In the meantime we discarded the topsail yards and became a fore and aft schooner with squaresail set flying from the deck. This meant I could make any passage without ballast.

We left Appledore for Newport, Monmouthshire, in high hopes and my mother, father and Captain H. Clarke of Braunton, who was agent for the maker of the engine, came with us. It was now September and the year had been very unremunerative for me sailing by the share, I had earned practically nothing for the whole year and had had plenty of hard work, but more trouble was to follow. The engine was found to be most unsatisfactory. It could only be run dead slow, and if speed of the revolutions was increased the engine would stop in less than twenty minutes, but after being stopped for thirty minutes would start again. Captain Clarke decided to draw the piston which was found to have a crack in it which allowed it to expand in the cylinder. A new piston was ordered and after laying a month at Newport we sailed for Clonakilty.

Now the installation of machinery and controls made it imperative for the compass to be adjusted and although I strongly objected to sailing without having the compass adjusted I was overruled by my father and sailed without anything being done. I got to Clonakilty fairly quickly and loaded oats for Gloucester. I got to Kingroad, off Avonmouth, and decided to go on up through the Shutes. I must admit I was rather early, but quite confident, but a combination of circumstances including fog and over-confidence brought on worse trouble than ever. It was just before daylight and I steered the usual course north north east from the Cockburn buoy intending to pick up the leading lights, but I just couldn't find them. Realising something was wrong I turned around in the opposite direction, intending to wait for daylight, when the engine stopped suddenly without warning; there was no wind to sail and I knew I was well up to Shutes. I jumped below to start the engine and it went each time for a few seconds, but time was passing and we were drifting. Suddenly she struck rocks, stopped a few minutes only, and dropped into deep water again; the engine started up and without further trouble continued until we arrived at Sharpness. We motored to Gloucester and when the cargo was out, put the ship in dry dock for examination, I found the keel gone from end to end and the sternpost broken and my heart well nigh broken, too. The repairs eventually cost five hundred pounds which was a big sum in those days.

My father came to Gloucester and I asked him to sell it all up and let me clear out. He refused to listen. We effected temporary repairs and Father remained on board while we ran a few cargoes of barbed wire to Briton Ferry from Gloucester. Of course I was condemned as a darned fool by Father because of my incompetence. I may have been to blame to some extent, but I felt it was unjust to lay it all on me. However, I bided my time and said nothing until one trip we approached the Shutes under exactly similar circumstances to when the damage occurred. We steered north north east from the Cockburn buoy and Father at the wheel in charge. This time the engine didn't stop and I waited. Suddenly Father shouted, " Can you see the leading lights ? " I replied, " No, can you ? ", and he was certainly puzzled. He turned her round and repeated in detail all I had done but we did have the engine going. Finally I said to Father, " I can tell you where you have gone wrong if you will listen to me. You have steered north north east across, but you are a long way to the westward, let her go away to the eastward and you will see the leading lights. Your compass is two points out on a northerly course, and now perhaps you will agree to have it adjusted." He found I was right and he admitted it was not all my fault.

To explain this I would add that previous to these happenings neither Father nor myself had been up the river Severn for several years and whilst away the Chepstow shipyards had been built, of which we had no knowledge. As we were off our course too far west the leading lights of Charstone and Oares were mixed up with the glaring electric lights at Chepstow shipyards and invisible to us. It never happened again because the compass was adjusted without further delay. We brought the ship home for Christmas and immediately after the holidays she was dry docked to renew the keel and sternpost.

We spent several weeks in dock and I well remember the date we left Appledore to start another year, as this was my mother's birthday, January 22nd. I had got over the troubles of the previous year and looked forward to a fresh start. I remember my youngest sister quoting a verse which helped to cheer me up during my somewhat gloomy despondency. I think the cost of that mistake of mine had got me worried as well as the managing owner. The verse ran like this, " It's all very well to be happy when life goes along like a song. But the person worth while is the one who can smile when everything goes dead wrong." And now it was up to me to see it went dead right.

We left for Lydney, chartered to load for Falmouth. When we got to Lydney our cargo wasn't ready and we had a few days to wait. A little steamer had failed to arrive to pick up a cargo waiting on the tip, and I was asked by the harbourmaster if I could take it to Ilfracombe, the freight being eleven shillings per ton, which was good. Permission had to be obtained from the coal controller at Bristol. This was granted, but I had to guarantee to complete the trip and be back for Falmouth in four days. I agreed and hauled under the tip immediately. I communicated with Father explaining the position and sailed that evening. It was dark when we got to Barry and blowing a gale. We carried on double reefed on the port tack. About midnight the foresail burst. We stowed it and kept going under motor power. After a wild night we arrived at Ilfracombe. I was rather washed out, as I had my first child's ailment, mumps ! It was very uncomfortable, to say the least.

Now Father had been sailing us along in his imagination and kept telling Mother where I ought to be. He hoped I wasn't on Penarth mud waiting for fine weather and it got Mother a little annoyed as she knew it was wild weather. When my telegram got home she took it in and kept it in her pocket. All that day Father was looking for a wire that never came. In the evening I walked in and I created a surprise, but he was, of course, pleased to see me and I went on to explain that we had a wild night. Our foresail was burst, but not beyond repair, and I could do it myself. He criticised me for not sending a telegram and I replied, " I did. We are discharging and I telegraphed this morning." Then Mother produced the telegram and said innocently, " Well this must be the one you were expecting, I got it early this morning." And then she pulled his leg to her heart's content. " It's all very well," he said, " but I've been worrying all day. I know it blew a gale last night and I shouldn't have been surprised if he had been on the mud and then lost the other cargo. We've lost enough lately and it's time some of the leeway was made up ! " We got back to Lydney on the fourth day, in time to collect the first cargo for Falmouth. We got round there very quickly, in fact from that time onward I did remarkably well, paying off the five hundred pounds debt with a substantial balance in the bank at the end of six months.

Then one day I fell in with an old mate of my father's days. I had been to sea with him as a little schoolboy and we were of course good friends. He was now master of the schooner *Camborne*. He asked how I had sustained the accident which caused so much damage. I told him the facts and added that Father had been very much upset over it and more than ever over my obvious incompetence. He replied, " You are not the only one to hit Groggy [the name of the rock]. There are plenty of Appledore men who have done that and been lucky to get away with little or no damage ! " He mentioned several ships which had lost keels and one of my father's own vessels, the *Saint Agnes* lost in the Severn driving up over the Lloyd rocks. He did me good, and helped me to recover my confidence.

I consider these voyages early in 1920 were really the start of my life in an auxiliary motor vessel, and bearing in mind that the master was also the engineer it can be understood life was no bed of roses. Whilst in harbour there was always plenty to do in the engine room besides having to work the cargoes in and out. The accommodation aft was crude and living conditions miserable, because half of the cabin was taken for engine room space and the smell of diesel oil was everywhere. There was no sleep at sea because of the excessive vibration and noise. Often the top of the flimsy deck house leaked like a colander, in fact, for twenty years I hardly knew what it was to have a dry bed to sleep in when away from home. In addition, being rather addicted to sea sickness I suffered badly from this for all the remainder of my life at sea, so how could I be expected to love it ? To me it was my living, and I did what I could to make it successful, but only I know how miserable I often felt during the time at sea and how I fought against the desire to lay windbound as often as I could.

But I did make a success of it all the way through and never allowed anyone to leave me behind, and I certainly didn't allow my sea sickness to hinder my chances of making a passage. There was one difference made through having motor power. It was not necessary to buy stocks of food and instead of salt beef our diet could be improved. The days of hunger had gradually passed, and even though conditions were so crude, there was plenty of good substantial food. In former days of sail the work started at

Plate 11.   *Grahame Farr*
    The ketch *Trio* of which W. J. Slade was master at the end of the first world
war.

Plate 12.   *National Maritime Museum*
    The old Quay from the west. The sailing barge alongside was called the
Mirre. The hulk was the brigantine *Oak*.

Plate 13. *National Maritime Museum*
The ketch *Margaret*, owned by Jack Lamey, a sailmaker, outward bound down the channel from Appledore to the bar. The man standing on the beach is Thomas Powe, who earned a living as a winchman discharging vessels.

Plate 14. *National Maritime Museum*
John Cann, Samuel Berry and John Cawsey, gravel bargemen, yarning on the Quay. The bows of the ketch *Emu* and the stern of the ketch *Advance* are also in the picture.

6 a.m. in harbour and finished at 6 p.m., if you were lucky. In the Irish ports, discharging by hand winch started at six and we worked to nine without a bite of food, and then sat down to breakfast of salt fish, bread and margarine. Dinner was at 2 p.m. with boiled salt beef and vegetables boiled all in the same pot, no tea after and no sweets. Then at 6 p.m. you finished working cargo and had tea, sometimes a small portion of the salt beef and tea with bread and margarine. If there was sufficient cold beef left from the previous dinner to make a dinner for the next day, you had to be satisfied with bread and margarine, or perhaps bread and jam for tea. But those days were happy because conditions were hard everywhere and we knew no different life. It was all changed during the first world war, better freights made better food possible and the coming of motors improved food conditions more than ever.

I think the year 1920 was the hardest and most remunerative of my life. One voyage to Cherbourg stands out in my memory. I had a good mate, who was considered a fine sailor. My brother was ordinary seaman, and a man who had spent his life in schooners was cook and able seaman. The latter was a little short chap who had a great opinion of himself. He caused a lot of amusement. We had driven the ship very hard against a strong south west wind and had got about six miles off Godrevy lighthouse, which is situated on the north Cornish coast. We were under reefed mainsail and in a heavy squall it fairly howled. We had to heave another reef in the mainsail as her lee rails were in the water. Now Tiny was on the winch handle turning it to heave down the reef and being the leeside he was up to his knees in water. He suddenly slipped and went down face under water, the mate put his foot on him. The mate said it saved Tiny from going out through the wash leaf, but I think he did it to terrify him. Tiny yelled enough for a dozen men and, when he recovered himself, in his excitement he threw off his oilskins and they immediately blew away and were never seen again. He always very emphatically stated after this that the *Millom Castle* washed a suit of oilskins clean off his back.

The mate had been continually suggesting we ought to run back for shelter, but I just felt I must get round the Longships and I'm afraid my determined attitude made the mate pretty miserable. About 4 p.m. the wind suddenly veered north west and the mate said, " Now you will have to go back," but I knew the *Millom Castle* better than he did and I replied " Not on your life."

We put her head down along and just before dark we were in a nice berth off Pendeen and in a position to weather the Longships. We had not had a meal all day, in fact there was no fire to cook anything with. The galley was well washed out and not a dry thread anywhere. We were all well washed with salt water, but I knew she would do it. Suddenly someone suggested a glass of whisky would go down well and I said, " Certainly, take a bottle out of my cupboard and have a glass each." They did so and my brother took his glass too. Then they thought of me stood at the wheel wet and cold. My brother knew I was a teetotaller but asked me to have a glass saying it would do me good. At first I refused but then gave in and asked for one with plenty of water in it. I ought to have known there was no water in the cabin, but I had my mind fully occupied looking after the ship and watching the steering. They passed a large glass to me and I drank it. It nearly took my breath away. I had never tasted it before and I felt it creep all over me, warming every inch of my body. I felt equal to anything, in fact as I found out later it was neat whisky and I was half intoxicated. Well never mind, it did me the world of good and I didn't feel any ill effects afterwards. . . .

We continued our trading through the summer months without any particular incident, doing good work all the year until winter set in. I had now settled my little family in at Bideford after having bought one house, which I could not occupy as the tenant refused to quit, and then another as alternative occupation. I therefore determined to trade home for the winter. During these voyages the mate often referred to the voyage when I first drank whisky. He freely admitted he completely had the wind up and how, when the wind had veered north west he said to the crew, " We'll have sand in our eyes before dark tonight ! " But, after it was over, he said, " I'll never be afraid of this old box again. She's ugly to look at, but she is a marvellous old craft."

We managed to keep on the run from Appledore to Bristol or Cardiff with gravel and home to Bideford with coal for the remainder of 1920 and well into 1921. I spent quite a lot of time home on these short trips and hardly ever had a night out, because we usually left home in the morning and would be in Bristol or Cardiff in the evening, thanks to motor power. When we left Lydney we couldn't get home in one tide, but we often anchored for the night either at Portishead or Penarth Roads, leaving next morning and being home in the evening. This of course was governed by tides and weather, but we had very few nights at sea during the whole winter and it was an easy one for me. The trade was usually run by smaller ships and we were looked upon by some, and I suppose with some justice, as interlopers, so when someone cut the freight from ten shillings to eight shillings and sixpence per ton I made up my mind to clear out again and leave the field clear for the smaller ships.

Our coastal trips continued all the summer of 1921 without any incident beyond the normal routine, but when September came it was found our mainsail required some considerable repairs and we made up our minds to rig the *Millom Castle* into a ketch. I think this was not a very wise move, but we still did a lot of sailing and the motor was stopped to save oil whenever the winds made it possible. We considered ourselves sailing ships and the engine was a secondary asset used mostly in an emergency or in calm weather. Therefore we rigged her in every respect as a sailing ketch and she answered very well under sail with quite a good turn of speed.

This was the last time I ever saw shear legs used for lifting out the lower masts. We stripped her down to the deck in one day. The mainmast used as a schooner was the bigger of the two masts and this was shifted forward as the mainmast of the newly rigged ketch and the foremast was poled off for a mizzen mast. We had the fore yard left from her topsail schooner days and this made a topmast. The whole job cost about ten pounds; cost of altering sails was additional to this figure.

When we started as a ketch my father came with us. His excuse was he wanted to see how she acted as a result of our work. As a sailing vessel she was certainly a great success, but she was a worse sea boat and wore out a lot more gear. She did not run many years as a ketch and during that period was dismasted, but this was after I had left her. Finally, after I had rerigged the ketch *Haldon* as a three masted fore and aft schooner in the way described later in this chapter, Father, to avoid the heavy costs of running a big ketch, had the *Millom Castle* altered to three masts to make all the sails smaller. To my annoyance he did not scarph the mainmast with the result that her appearance was odd in the extreme and some wag at Appledore nicknamed her " The set of jugs." This rig, which can be seen in the photograph of her in this book (Plate 16), despite its oddity proved efficient and the ship would work very well under sail alone without the engine. She remained this way as long as we had her.

Father stayed with us for several trips, and, of course, had his wages as one of the crew, in fact he considered he was worth more than the rest of us, but we didn't disagree, and he finally left us when the cold weather set in. Freights had all gone down and I felt they were as low as possible. I was wrong in this.

At this period I worked out a system to work by the share with the crew, and I am the only one who ever tried this. The ship's third was paid to the owners as usual and the remaining two thirds shared as follows:—The costs of oil for running the engine and all food and port expenses were first deducted from the two thirds and the balance put into eleven shares and divided between myself and the crew. The crew now consisted of the mate, one able seaman and myself. I took four shares the mate four shares and the able seaman took three shares. By way of extra remuneration as master, I received all thirds of chartering commission amounting to approximately twenty-five shillings per cargo, plus two guineas gratuity if the charter had gratuity included in it. In those days this was a recognised thing, payable to all masters. The scheme worked perfectly until I left the ship some eighteen months or so after. The crew did well because extra voyages meant extra money and, owning part of the ship, the benefit of our extra work came to me in several different ways.

The *Millom Castle* continued to pay handsomely all through the period I sailed in her. Cargoes began to get more scarce, but we worked hard together and often put in many hours extra. The clock was never considered, as long as there was work to do we did it night or day. On one occasion I was in Bristol discharging clay into barges. I had to go to Briton Ferry light to load coal out, when I got a message to say that if I could get to Portishead the following morning I could load a cargo of grain for Swansea. This meant about £80 to handle between us, instead of nothing. The bugbear was we had fifty tons of cargo left in the hold and tide time was 8 a.m. The men had left work, but an empty barge was alongside and there was no one to stop us from loading her. We worked all that night, three of us shovelled it in the ship's hold, hove it up with the winch, tipped it into the barge and trimmed the barge too, good work for three men only. When the shore gang came to start work we were leaving the wharf to catch the tide out of Bristol. I told them I would pay the full money to them, but it appears I had broken union rules and they threatened to stop my ship from leaving, but I got out before they could act and was loading the grain that day. I never heard any more about it, so it worked out pretty good for us.

On another occasion we were at Appledore windbound for Penryn. One evening it seemed to moderate so, as it had a fortnight to Christmas, we agreed to try to get round the Longships and if successful we hoped to get back for Christmas. On rounding Hartland point we found a strong southerly wind. We took in our topsail and reefed down, heading down channel on the port tack, but not laying our course. It looked forbidding, but as we were out I determined we wouldn't give up easily. My cousin met us in the *Progress*, bound to the Bristol Channel, he came close enough to shout and warned us of a strong wind below, adding, " You won't do much with it." Well, we carried on and the next morning were about ten miles off St. Ives when the wind veered westerly and we weathered the Longships easily. It was certainly a stroke of luck, and better still it threw us into a round of good fortune hard to believe possible. We discharged our cargo, loaded grain overnight for Swansea and the grain merchants gave the men £1 each gratuity. We left and arrived at Swansea the next evening, discharged right away under the elevator, sailed for Avonmouth loaded maize for Padstow, discharged at Padstow, left for Bridgwater light and loaded bricks for Bideford. We finished discharging the bricks on Christmas Eve. The crew were delighted to pick up their well earned Christmas packet and I was equally on top of the world with plenty of cash to make Christmas worth while for my family.

Nineteen hundred and twenty-two opened with much the same outlook, we carried on our trade as usual till February found us on passage to Clonakilty in the County of Cork. This voyage was an unfortunate one from a financial point of view, but I may say I am lucky to be writing this today after all we went through. We got to Clonakilty after a struggle, but this is a bad harbour and fine weather is essential for getting in and out of it. It has a very shallow and very narrow approach, only wide enough to admit one ship at a time. The distance across from the barrel rock in the entrance to the sand bank bar is approximately thirty feet to forty feet and our beam was twenty-one feet. The sea breaks very heavily in strong southerly and south westerly winds even at

F

high water, and the maximum depth of water at spring tides is only about thirteen feet.

Well, we got in and the elements shut the door. We were locked in with bad weather for weeks. We discharged our coal and loaded the last cargo of barytes to come out of that place. I must explain that this commodity is used for making white lead, or so I was told. It is very heavy stuff and extremely hard on any ship as the hold isn't half full although in weight the whole cargo is contained in this small quantity, and in consequence a ship caught in bad weather will easily strain and this in a wood ship means leaking and probably pumping continually for many hours. It certainly needs a strong ship to carry it and I intended to show that the *Millom Castle* could do it as well as any other.

After we finished loading I rove off a new set of hemp lanyards throughout to make sure the mast would be well stayed up. We left towards the end of February and put into Kinsale windbound where we remained until March 7th with continual gales blowing. The wind had veered north west on the 7th and still blowing hard, but as it appeared to be set that way, and being a fair wind I decided to sail. We ran about eighty miles under reefed canvas, but I noticed the weather glass tumbling down and before dark made sure everything on deck was well secured. I even doubled the mizzen reef pennants. Shortly after this we ran into a calm and we started the engine to try to get into the entrance to the Bristol Channel before the gale, which was evidently coming, could break on us, but in less than an hour we ran into the full force of a south south easterly gale. Soon a nasty cross sea came up. The heavy westerly sea was running over the lee quarter and the south south easterly sea rising heavier all the time made it a proper inferno.

The wind was gradually backing easterly and about midnight I decided making bad weather of it. We lay all night practically hove to, the sea like mountains and wind gradually working round eastward to a northerly point. When dawn broke she looked awful, water breaking on board in huge quantities, which made me wonder if she could possibly stick any more, but she was tight, staunch and strong. She made no water so we hadn't got to pump. About 10 a.m. the sea seemed to be running true and after discussing the matter we agreed that if we could run her for twenty miles she may ease the sea and so get inside the line of the Smalls situated off the Pembroke coast.

We ran lovely for about half an hour, when a huge sea broke over the port quarter, the helm seemed useless, she was full to the top of the rails. In the hollow of the sea the main boom came in and when it went out it broke in two, the gaff went in three pieces. The boat's gripes had broken and she was afloat on the sea. When the ship recovered the boat fell across the lee rail and balanced in on deck. The battens and hatch wedges were adrift and one end of main hatch tarpaulin off. The fore end of the main boom with heavy iron patent reef attached was over the side, towing. It was sheering off and coming in hitting the side of the ship threatening to drive through her like a battering ram. Other running gear was washed overboard, tangling in the propellor which finished the engine. The mainsail, of course, disappeared altogether.

Then the fight started. My brother and the mate, who was my cousin, secured the boat and the boom, and then nailed the battens and tarpaulins to the hatch combings to keep the water out. Most of this time they were waist deep in water. I had to steer her dead before the gale, under bare poles. All that day we kept running and the boat, lashed to the lee rails, never once showed herself clear of the water. My crew was marvellous. My brother was only seventeen, and where the mate went to do a job, he, too, was there to help. They were like two drowned rats, but never once did they despair. We were heading for Pendeen and about 5 p.m. we picked it up on the port bow. I planned to run close around the Longships and try to get a bit of sail on her to get her in a bit of smoother water so that I could do something with some spare sails, but it was not to be. When we got Pendeen well up and we were abreast St. Ives, the wind suddenly backed west north west and we were caught on a lee shore.

I think my mate had had enough; he was worn out. He suggested St. Ives Bay and the lifeboat to take us off. I thought for a few minutes and then said, " No, I won't lose the vessel while she will stay afloat." We wore her round with her head to the north east which brought the sea on her port bow. We set the whole mizzen after hooking the mizzen mast head tackle forward to an eyebolt in the deck. This supported the mast head, and prevented it from going over the stern with the excessive strain on it. Then we hooked the main topping lift back to support the main mast head, setting the boom jib, which was a new sail. Then we set the whole staysail. After we had trimmed these to suit the conditions I looked over the stern and when I saw she was carrying her wake straight astern my spirits rose considerably because I knew she would weather up Trevose and possibly Hartland point.

All that night the sea broke over her in continual heavy volumes, we tried her pumps each watch, but she was as sound as a bell. It was really wonderful for an old wooden ship built in 1870 to stand up to such buffeting with a very heavy cargo and remain absolutely tight. I felt proud of the old box. She was ugly, but as good as gold and I felt sure, as long as our remaining sails held, she would see us through. The next day we sighted Lundy and after passing up with a good offing I kept away for the Bristol Channel. We now had the wind behind us and set the squaresail, after reefing it. It was on her about fifteen minutes when the yard broke in the middle, so down it came again. The weather was now moderating fast and by the time we were off the Hangman Point, the sea had gone and we were able to take stock of our position. The local steamer *Woolston* came along, saw our wrecked condition and offered assistance, which was declined with thanks. It was nearly dark again and our navigation lights were washed away so we fitted up the " out of control " red lamp on port side and the anchor lamp on the other side, shaded by some green material.

Then we tackled the propellor. We grappled up the ropes that were towing behind still tangled in the propellor and led them to our hand winch. By working the flywheel of the engine in gear just a little and heaving in on the winch we gradually got a few inches of rope and the more we got the more I could move the propellor. After an hour of patient struggle we got a full revolution of the propellor and I made up my mind to start the engine. I put the clutch in suddenly to see if it would break clear. To my great satisfaction, after a second or two, it cleared itself and we motored past Barry and finally anchored off Portishead safe. We laid down completely fagged out till 7 a.m. then lighted a fire to make a cup of tea. We had had practically nothing to eat and nothing to drink for three days and nights. When the tea was made, we couldn't drink it, because our drinking water was salt. We just wet our lips, hove up the anchor and proceeded up the Avon to Bristol, feeling half dead.

But even now our troubles were not over. It is usual to enter the river four hours flood, and a pontoon is stationed outside

Cumberland Basin to allow inward traffic to moor alongside if the entrance is not clear. The pontoon was full up with craft, who were unable to get in because a big American steamer was blocking the entrance. We had to stop against the mud bank just below the pontoon. This we managed all right, but the steamer after clearing the locks went full ahead and her propellor sucked our stern off, and parted our stern rope, which went under and tangled our propellor again. We turned round stern up river and we were again in trouble. A dredger came along and towed us in the locks for ten shillings. When we got halfway in I shouted, " Let go ! Fast enough." The dockmaster counter-manded my order, saying, " Hang on that tow rope, it's not enought yet," but we couldn't stop her, it was too fast and we ran into a barge doing some damage, which was not serious.

The dockmaster knew he was wrong; he just disappeared. Well, by this time my brain was in a whirl. I telegraphed home " Arrived badly damaged." I hardly knew what I was doing and it seemed now that nothing mattered. We got to our discharging berth, begged some fresh water, made tea with a snack or two to eat and went to bed. The next day Father appeared on the scene and when he saw the state our ship was in he said, " Good God ! How in the world did she come through it ? " The salt had corroded in the eyes of her rigging forty feet above the deck. The first words Father said to me were, " Never mind the damage, that's nothing. The wind registered one hundred and eight miles an hour at the Scilly Isles during the gale and you were not expected to live through it with such a heavy cargo."

Well, we soon cleared up the mess, a mainsail belonging to the *Progress* was kindly sent to us by my uncle to bring us home, where a new one was being made. We bought the spars of a ketch called *Janette* which was being broken up and we had them cheap. We loaded manure for Bideford and to clear the propellor we loaded the fore end first so that we could just reach the propellor to clear it. Father left by train for home and the next day we followed in our ship. There was quite a lot of talk about the *Millom Castle* and how she weathered out that gale and it was somewhat of a coincidence that the blizzard of 1891, which started on March 8th, was a critical time in my father's life. He was driven down on the Cornish coast in the little ketch *Francis Beddoe* with a dead-weight capacity of only seventy tons and saw a bitter time; he never expected to return, but he came back and lived to own several coasters, which shows what these small sailing ships are capable of withstanding.

On looking back over my ordeal I feel I erred in one thing: I should have been satisfied to remain hove to till the gale abated instead of taking the risk of running her. I am quite sure, however, that she would have run comfortably had she been a topsail schooner. A ketch is not a good rig to run in a gale, in fact I prefer a topsail schooner any time in any bad weather conditions. That voyage and the hard ordeal we passed through will always remain in my memory as the most critical and dangerous voyage in my whole life.

In July 1922 we purchased the ketch *Haldon* 175 tons. I left the *Millom Castle* to take charge of her, and went to Haverfordwest with my father to take her to Appledore for survey to insure with the Braunton Shipowner's Mutual Insurance Association. She had a very heavy mainsail as a ketch and Father and I had hard work to set it. It was a double barrel winch job from the commencement of the operation, but we finally arrived home in safety. After a few days we chartered with clay for London and back to Bideford with cement. My brother came with me and a young man from Ilfracombe who made himself useful with the engine, a great asset, as driving the engine was a job no one cared for when at sea.

My father made up his mind to have a voyage or two in the *Haldon* to test her out. She was a handy ship under sail, but I didn't like her. She was not only weak in construction but a dirty brute at sea. However, earning power counted most and she was economical to run, so I had to make the best of her bad qualities and take the good with the bad. Altogether I did quite well with her and after 28 years sold her for double the price we paid for her.

We left Appledore about July 20th and as our ship had been laid up for a long period at Haverfordwest the running gear wasn't much good. We opened out Hartland Point. The wind was south-west, fresh, and the gear started to give out, so we got back to anchor in Clovelly Roads where we started repairs. and after an hour or two seemed to be all tidy again. We sailed early next morning with light winds about west and a nasty sea. I spent a good many hours during the time we were going down the north Cornish coast, reeving new running gear and repairing some of the breakages. I was glad to be round the corner to run up the English Channel in comfort. It wasn't long before Father wanted to sail. He said every time the engine fired it cost a halfpenny and he counted all those puffs of vapour coming out of the exhaust pipe, saying it was a woeful waste of money. In the end he had his way and we sailed along quite comfortably, averaging about six knots. It came dirty south-west by the time we got to Anvil Point, so it was decided to run up inside the Isle of Wight for the night, anchoring off Cowes.

I upset the owner a little when I told him we couldn't all afford to go yachting, so the next morning he got up early and hurried us all to get going again. However, we did have a very nice trip and finally arrived in Cherry Garden Tier London, where we discharged into barges. After discharging we shifted to Swanscombe and were soon on our way out again. We had a lovely north north-west wind all the way down channel and after three days, sailing nearly all the way, we arrived at Bideford.

There I expected Father would leave us, but, oh no, he wanted mother to make a trip and I found myself going over the bar a few days later as a passenger ship, with my mother and sister added to the list. Of course mother enjoyed it, she was a good sailor and could adapt herself to conditions as she found them.

We got to Lydney the next day and loaded for Gweek. This is a very shallow place about six or seven miles above Helford and frequented by barges. We got a pilot at Helford but stuck in the river about a quarter of a mile from the quay. This was not the fault of the pilot, she was in the proper channel but there wasn't water enough even with a high spring tide, but Father had been there several times before and he said: " We'll soon lighten her ! " I said, " Which way ? " " Oh," he said, " there were barges here, years ago." When we started counting back to his day, I found that was twenty years ago, and I said: " Some hopes." He said: " We'll up in the boat," and sure enough we found an old condemned barge, just about hanging together, but she was sunk. Well, we got her freed of water as the tide went out, chinked up all the seams and bad places with oakum and on the next tide dropped her down the river alongside our ship, took out about 15 tons from the after hatch, which was all we dared to put in the barge in her rotten condition, floated it up to the quay alongside of our ship and hove it out of her before the barge had time to sink.

Well, we discharged, and although we ordered our pilot, he didn't come, so Father said: " Let go the ropes, I'll take her down the river." On the way down we had to encounter some nasty bends. I was at the wheel taking orders from the self-appointed pilot, who stood on the knightheads, shouting his orders. My brother was standing by me and I said to him in an ordinary tone: " I don't believe he knows where he is going." And Father snapped back from nearly a hundred feet away: " Oh don't I ? You do as you are told." We both looked at each other and laughed. He was over sixty and his hearing was wonderful. Well he took her down all right and we never touched anywhere. He certainly had a good memory after over twenty years away from that river.

We chartered from Par to Runcorn which meant going from Helford empty. Mother had gone home but we couldn't get rid of Father. He was enjoying himself and he didn't want to go home till the weather got colder. . . .

We made a good run to Runcorn, but the next thing I knew the owner had chartered her for Gweek again. I wasn't too pleased about this, but it had to be faced, so we settled down to make the best of it. When we left we encountered a strong south-west wind and went to Holyhead windbound. We laid there four or five days comfortably enough, but Father got up about 5.30 every morning and made a monotonous walk to and fro over my head till I had to get out of bed. Every few minutes he'd stop and knock out his pipe. Where I slept, my head was only about two feet from the deck; so Father's walk sounded like hammers, so he naturally got what he wanted. I was glad to get up and he would look so injured if I grumbled. When we left Holyhead it was still a head wind we had to face and, of course, the engine was stopped. Father again was saving those halfpennies. Personally I didn't care twopence which way it was, but my brother was very dissatisfied with it all.

Now Father was a slave to his pipe and when at the wheel he had to smoke. George smoked cigarettes and had a good stock, while Father's stock wasn't so good, so George was determined to work Father's stock out as quickly as he could. He would lean against the wheelhouse alongside of Father and his coat pocket, the top of which was wide open with so much use. He would slip his hand in Father's pocket very quietly and take some tobacco to make cigarettes. George was good pals with Father all the time the tobacco lasted and his fingers slipped in Father's pocket at every opportunity. At last Father said: " My bacca has gone awfully quick. I seem to have used double the usual quantity." At last came the request: " Give me a cigarette George." And the innocent reply came: " Haven't you got some in stock, Father ? " Father said: " No, I seem to have used the lot." " Well, at the rate we are going, my cigarettes won't last half way," says George. " Why not start up the engine and get somewhere to replenish your stock ? " Father says: " We will when your cigarettes are gone, go down and get me one." George said: " I'm not going to risk being caught short, but if you have the engine started I'm willing to go fifty-fifty." " Right," says Father, after some more futile arguments. " Start her up ! " and we did. Then Father said: " I want my half now, come on." " Not that way," says George. " We'll share equally, every time I have a smoke you'll have one as well." George had no flies on him, he suspected that if Father had half all at once, he would have the engine stopped again. But the engine was kept going till our arrival and the cigarettes lasted the voyage. Father never found out about his tobacco till years after and we all enjoyed the fun, doing our best to attract Father's attention while the robbery was on. I'm afraid George could always handle Father better than me. . . .

On another occasion Father was making a few voyages with George in the *Millom Castle*. They got to Milford during a run of very wild weather conditions. There was quite a crowd of ships lying quietly on Angle mud, but Father kept the *Millom Castle* off afloat. Every morning regularly they hoisted the sails and got under way to go to sea, went as far as St. Ann's, or the islands off Milford, and back again. It worried the other ships till they finally got used to it and took it as a matter of course. One day he went ashore and the question was asked him: " Why do you keep on going in and out ? " He replied: " I'm teaching the crew how to handle a sailing ship. All they want nowadays is motors." Needless to say he never once started the engine and George said: " All right Father, you carry on, you seem to be captain." When they got to their destination, Ballycotton, they finished discharging. Now the consignee was a generous type of man and always gave some allowance in cash to the crew; Father, of course, as the mate, was entitled to his share, but George picked up the cash, and when Father asked for his share, George replied: " You can't have it both ways Father, you've got to pay for the privilege of being captain."

Well, to resume our second voyage to Gweek in the *Haldon*, we got right up to the quay on the top of a high spring tide and during our stay there, one of our ships, the *Heather Bell*, was caught in Coverack in an easterly gale. This ship was owned by my uncle T. Slade and Father. She parted all her moorings, and a phone message came from her master for assistance. We loaded a lorry up with big hausers which we carried on board *Haldon*, took them to Coverack and remoored the *Heather Bell*. We also used the chain cables, but she went through the lot after pulling all the big granite posts out and some of the quay with them. She eventually went ashore just outside the piers on rocks the north side of the harbour and became a total wreck. Father went home and the mate of *Heather Bell* joined the *Haldon*, where he continued for quite a long time.

After a few months' trading round the coasts of Ireland and London districts the master of the *Millom Castle*, Captain Charles White, whose only daughter became the wife of one of my sons years afterwards, decided to leave his ship, much to our regret. And this meant the former master of *Heather Bell* went in her taking his former mate who was his son, out of the *Haldon* leaving the berth in the latter vacant. My brother was now old enough and good enough to take the position as mate, so we shipped an old friend of my father's, who had been many years master in schooners and ketches, as cook and able seaman. He preferred this position, as he wanted to take life quietly. We did our best to see that he did not work too hard. I had a deep respect for the old man, as he was mate with Father when I was little more than a baby and I had sailed with him many voyages. We were certainly a happy ship in those days with my brother, the old former skipper, and a decent young Ilfracombe chap as ordinary seaman.

After a few more voyages the *Haldon* received weather damage on a voyage to Bridgwater. The gaff topsail burst and we had to send it down on deck for repairs which the mate and I managed all right, but she was a heavy ketch and served her sails and gear bad if we met any hard weather. In addition I found the mainmast was slightly rotten in the eyes of the rigging, which meant lifting the rigging and trestle trees to thoroughly examine it. I got in communication with my father on the matter and we agreed to load bricks for Bideford where the examination could take place.

After discharge we shifted to Harris' Yard, Appledore, when we found a new mast was required if she remained a ketch. I got busy with my rule and drafted out the *Haldon* rigged as a three masted fore and aft schooner, with pole masts. As the mainmast was a seventeen inch spar we could reduce it to fourteen inch and take out all the rot by poling it off on top, hounding the rigging down several feet and tonguing the heel. This was now the fore mast with a fifteen foot pole above the eyes of the rigging. When the mizzen mast was lifted out to be shifted further aft this too was found bad, but as the mizzen would be smaller it was reduced till it was good. It remained only to find a mainmast and main gaff and boom to go in the middle of the ship and she was a handy three-masted schooner. The sails were cut to fit and three gaff topsails supplied. She was a great success, sailed well and handled well, light as well as loaded. Her gear lasted three times longer and she was a far better sea boat. The cost of rigging was saved in three years by the easy motion in bad weather in a sea way. The only sail missing was a squaresail to run before the wind. This was soon remedied. We had a spare sail on board which was formerly a schooner's fore and aft foresail. It was cut square across from the jaws of the gaff (or cringle in the weather rope) to the leech, a bonnet or three-cornered piece sewn on each side from the head down to nothing, which gave us a sail thirty feet on the head, twenty-two feet six inch on the foot, and the hoist about twenty-eight or twenty-nine feet.

We had one or two topsail yards spare and soon had a square sail yard and sail that we could set from the deck on a jack stay fitted foreside the mast from the trestle trees to the saddle. This sail was a wonderful help and we made many passages without using the motor at all. The photograph at Plate 17 shows the vessel as she was when we finished rerigging her.

As the months passed we did quite a lot of trade to London with pottery clay, which was a heavy cargo, but the rig made it a much easier job for the ship and lighter work for the crew. On one particular voyage I had to leave Par light for Penryn in order to pick up tin concentrates for London. The loading berth at Penryn was very shallow and it needed the top of a high spring tide to get out of it with a full cargo. It was only two days to the top of the spring and a strong south-west wind blowing up against us. The chances of getting down against it were slim indeed, but I determined to test her out and if I failed, to run back to Fowey. It was dark when we left, but for a ship with no ballast she was wonderful. She carried the three fore and afters and head sails as well as a loaded ship could do it and we anchored in Falmouth Harbour a few hours afterwards. When we got to Penryn on the next tide my ship-broker friend Mr N. S. Furneaux was agreeably surprised. He could not imagine how we had managed to get down in such adverse circumstances, but through this we had a quick turn round and a few days after discharged in London.

CHAPTER 5

THE DEPRESSION AND AN INTERLUDE IN SAIL AGAIN

IT WAS NOW the mid nineteen-twenties. Freights were getting scarce and it was gradually becoming more difficult to keep running. It was a case of survival of the fittest and the life became harder as the months rolled by. I think the next few years were about the worst in my experience, indeed the master was expected to drive the ship as engineer and also work cargo to make ends meet and the modern Dutch coaster, subsidised by the Dutch government, infiltrated into all our trade. Is it any wonder that our merchant service went to pieces, with British ships laid up in hundreds in every harbour and certificated deepwater masters obliged to beg for a berth before the mast?

If we earned any money the income tax authorities claimed their cut and often when the time came for B.O.T. survey we lived in dread of the expense forced on us. The small auxiliary sailing vessels were treated the same as a large ship would be, and often absolutely ridiculous regulations were imposed. I remember on one occasion we had to have a new boat. This had to pass B.O.T. regulations and when put to the use for which it was needed it proved absolutely useless, insomuch that I made one trip after passing B.O.T. loadline survey, sold the boat and the same boatbuilder at Appledore built me another in its place· allowing me back the same amount I had paid. The first boat was sold to a Dutch ship and, of course, was satisfactory for their purpose. The boatbuilder was a man who knew how to handle a boat as well as build one, but there was no chance of practical men persuading the theoretical ones that they were wrong, so we had to endure whatever they ordered. Often the rubbish to which we had to submit was kept stowed away and only brought to light when the survey was

Plate 15.   *National Maritime Museum*
    A ketch off the end of the Quay, towards the top of the tide, salmon boats in the foreground,

Plate 16.   *W. J. Slade*
             The *Millom Castle* as a " set of jugs."

Plate 17.   *The late Gerald White*
The *Haldon* when she was first rigged to W. J. Slade's design as a three-masted schooner.

Plate 18.   *National Maritime Museum*
A dozen vessels and several gravel barges lying side by side off Appledore Quay.

due, I can say, now that my shipowning days are over, that I knew better than any surveyor could possibly know, what vital repairs my ship needed and she went without those very necessary repairs simply because, after complying with B.O.T. regulations, we couldn't afford to do the vital ones so badly needed.

Who were the better qualified to know what was needed in these small coasters, the men who had sailed in them for generations and could handle small open boats almost as soon as they left off their baby clothes, or the bureaucrats who gave orders from offices and most of whom needed a lesson themselves in the handling of boats ? . . .

Once we took a cargo to Antwerp and back to Exeter from Willebroeck with a cargo of plate glass. Then on to Plymouth and back to the Bristol Channel where we loaded at Lydney for Ballinacurra in Cork Harbour. On the way down channel the engine suddenly stopped with an awful smash. When I went to see the cause I found the cylinder and crank-case gone and also the bottom part of the piston broken. I tried to think of a remedy but it seemed hopeless. It was a double cylinder engine and one half of it was broken or damaged. We were now off Swansea and my mate advised me to get across the channel and in over the bar for repairs. As usual we disagreed and I replied, " I've sailed it before and I can do it again, so we shall finish the voyage under sail ! "

Several days later we sighted the Irish coast off Dungaron, the sky looked bad and I felt we were in for a blow from a southerly point. I had been trying to study out how to work that smashed up engine, so after breakfast set about making it into a single cylinder engine. First I took off the after cylinder head and drew out the broken piston. I put it in the cylinder upside down, hanging it in a stationary position to block the exhaust ports, at the same time making sure the webs on the crankshaft would turn round clear of it. Then I blocked the water courses and disengaged the fuel pump on the broken cylinder, turning it round a few revolutions I now thought there was a chance it would work on one cylinder, but whether it would drive the propellor was another matter. Well, we started it up and away it went as a 25 b.h.p. motor instead of a 50 b.h.p., but when we put it in gear it stopped and failed to take up the load. Then we tried again and I arranged to have the clutch put in while I stood by the fuel pump and water injection to give it sufficient to drive the load. This time it took the load and I adjusted it, watching it closely for possible failures to develop, but it never stopped till we anchored in Cork Harbour the following midnight.

When tide time and daylight came to proceed up the river it refused to go, which set another problem, so we got under way and sailed up to our discharging berth. That night I couldn't sleep trying to solve the riddle as to why it went for at least twelve hours and now refused. Well at 1 a.m. I jumped to the solution and, although tired out, I got up to test out my theory and sure enough it started. I got back to bed and slept dead till 7 a.m. when we had to commence discharge of cargo. In due course we sailed for home to have our engine repairs done. The engine never stopped from Cork Harbour to Appledore and when we berthed Father asked what I was doing coming home for engine repairs. " There's nothing wrong," he said. I invited him to look down in the engine room and when he saw half of the engine hung up to the beams, he stopped a while and then he said: " It's working better than ever, and if you only work one cylinder you'll save money in fuel so you had better go on as it is ! " Of course we had a laugh, but Father couldn't see anything to laugh at, so he cleared out and left us.

The following day we stripped the engine down and put a patch on the crankcase, but it always leaked air in and was not a success. It seems idle to describe the patched up repairs which were definitely the world's champion in this respect, but from then until that engine was finally scrapped my life was almost unbearable, and we were often making voyages with only half of the engine working and the other half hung up to the beams. I bought several pairs of second-hand big end bearings because they were often running out and having to be re-metalled. I certainly was an expert in fitting new ones in. What caused this was that the damaged piston had been put in the lathe and turned down because it wouldn't go down in the repaired cylinder. I myself discovered, too late, why it wouldn't go down. We had a new gudgeon pin made and the fitter had made it a quarter of an inch too long, with the result that the scraper that gathered the oil from the cylinder wall was jamming the piston. This was put right and the piston fell in too slack for compression. It rattled, when working like a sack of mussels. In consequence the carbon would blow down through the piston rings, blocking the banjo oiler fastened on the webs and out would go the big end for lack of lubricating oil.

On one voyage to Moorhill Quay (Youghal river) I had to catch the spring tide. It was fine calm weather and the motor had to be kept going somehow. I fitted six big end bearings that trip, no sleep or rest for three days. I arrived in the evening, sent a telegram home from Youghal and then set to about the engine because it was our last tide up the river on the following day. I worked all that night stripping the engine to the shaft, cleaned the banjo oilers and built it up again. We got to our berth all right, but completely worn out body and soul.

Freights were low and it was a struggle to keep going. Just after this my mate decided to retire as he was entitled to the " old-age pension " and could pick up a little fishing to help make it do. I was left with two boys and I now arranged for a cousin to join me as mate, but he couldn't get to me for a week or two, and therefore sent his boy to fill the gap, so off I went to Lydney with the three lads, none of whom could take a watch and could only steer alone in fine weather. We sailed from Lydney to Clonakilty and it can easily be understood that sleep was out of the question as far as I was concerned, but we arrived all right and after discharging loaded oats for Newport. On leaving Clonakilty we got a strong northerly wind and I had to get the gaff topsail down. It fouled aloft and I had to put the best boy at the wheel while I went aloft to clear it. While aloft I had to watch the steering shouting orders when the ship was in danger of jibing. I was glad when I got on deck again and from then to our arrival never left the wheel.

It was now 1927 and freights were in a pretty bad way. We stayed principally in the Irish trade and I made up my mind to re-arrange the constitution of the crew. I had been sailing four-handed and after considerable thought on the matter I came to the conclusion it would be cheaper if I paid £1 per month extra to the mate and carried a good man before the mast as cook and able seaman. It would save the food of one and give me a little extra wages too. This, of course, depended on the co-operation of my crew, but they understood something had to be done to make ends meet. It worked very well and we were happy together for quite a while trading without much to relate, but always with engine trouble, and many miles and voyages were made under sail. . . .

In 1929 after repeatedly writing to Father asking for a bigger ship, the *M. A. James* was purchased for my brother George. Arrangements were also put in hand to purchase a new Ellwe engine for the *Haldon*, but we kept going until the new engine was delivered at Messrs. P. K. Harris yard for quick installation. We got home at Christmas time ready for this work to be carried out.

From the time the engine was ordered I drove the old one mercilessly and didn't care what happened to it. Strange to say we had less trouble during this period, although whenever we started it we never got it to start on the two cylinders, always having to lock the fuel pump on the poor one until there was compression enough to make it fire and it often went off with a rush when it did go, smoke and fumes everywhere.

It terrified my cousin Jack of the *Progress* but Jack wasn't the only one that had the wind up over that engine. I remember one occasion when my brother got Father up the pole. It was usual to inject fresh water on the bulbs attached to cylinder heads in order to cool them down. If allowed to get too hot the exhaust pipe would catch fire and the flame and sparks would fly in the air. It would really do it good, cleaning out the silencer beautifully, and this was a dirty job as a rule. Father had relieved me off the Lizard at midnight. He and my brother came on watch and my brother was responsible for driving the engine in that watch. George said to me: " If you hear any yelling don't turn out of bed unless I call you." About half an hour after that I knew what mischief he was up to because the engine eased down a bit. The next thing I heard was Father's voice: " Billie, jump up, we are all on fire." I'll swear the din could be heard a mile away as Father was roaring at the top of his voice. Well, I had to get out and soon put the water on and looked for George. He was lying on the deck splitting his sides with laughter and keeping out of sight.

Well, to get back to our new engine. I was very delighted to be having a new engine, but I was still very low powered. It was 64 b.h.p. Ellwe. I wanted a 90 b.h.p., but I owned only one-third of the ship and I was overruled. This meant I was often behind others in an engine race and I was forced to drive it hard to compete with those who had bigger power. It was a bad mistake, but I had to be content, although often at a disadvantage. The difference in price was £200 and in the long run I definitely proved right in my estimate. My oil bills were bigger than the others because of the extra motoring hours and hard driving, and the wear and tear was much greater on the engine parts.

We got home and were under carpenters about Christmas 1929. In the new year we surveyed the *M. A. James* and purchased her at Plymouth. My mate was put in charge of the *Millom Castle* and Father, my brother and I went to Plymouth after the *M. A. James*. The latter had been laid up a considerable time and all her running gear, sails, etc., were stored. Our agreement was that she should be put ready for sea at the seller's expense. A former mate who had sailed in her for a long period rigged her out with sails and running gear, and I was elected as master for the time being. I felt happy to be once again master of a fine double topsail schooner, but I had a hard enough time before we got her home. . . .

We towed down to Millbay Dock and took in our cargo, sailed on the Tuesday evening and arrived to Truro Wednesday morning, the last tide up the river. After discharging we towed to Falmouth. We were chartered to load stone at Porthoustock for Ilfracombe, but the wind had come strong easterly, so that made it impossible to load, because the loading berth is exposed to the whole English Channel with the wind in this direction. We spent our leisure time turning our new ship's lockers and store cupboards out and making certain adjustments. We didn't bother to reeve off any new gear, such as braces and topsail halyards, sheets, clewlines, and downhauls because we had an engine ready to install at Appledore and intended to send down the topsail yards when she became an auxiliary.

We spent a whole week at Falmouth before the weather moderated sufficiently to load. One morning we got on deck to find it quite calm. The tug came alongside and we decided we would try to get our cargo. When we got out under the cliffs there still seemed to be plenty of sea, but the tug was well fendered up alongside and in we went. We parted several mooring ropes but the skipper of the tug knew his job and gave us all possible assistance. We got our full cargo in, which took about one hour. It consisted of two hundred and five tons of granite road stone. The tug towed us clear of Porthoustock and let go our rope a nice berth off the Manacles. We got all the sails up and carried on for the Lizard. When we got down in Mount's Bay the wind steadily freshened in a north-east direction. We tried our pumps and found she was leaking badly. Owing to being laid up for two years her seams had opened and from then until we arrived to Ilfracombe we hardly left her pump. It was clearly a case for dry docking and caulking all over.

In the meantime Father suggested anchoring in Gwavas Lake, off Newlyn Piers, for the night hoping the seams would close and the ship tighten up. She did a little, but even then every half an hour we had to pump. Of course Father couldn't do much as he was sixty-five years of age and expected to be treated as a very old man, quite contrary to present day standards when men much older are

considered young. At last I got tired of pumping and keeping watch
to do it. I suggested we may be just as well off at sea pumping as
lying at anchor doing the same thing, so we got under way, wind
still north-east strong, and headed for the Longships.

Now we were told at Plymouth the *M. A. James* was a lovely
ship, her fault was she was so very slow, always arriving back
from the Mersey a day or two after all the others. Whether this
was true or not I don't know, but it became obvious at once that
she was far from being a slow ship and indeed when we put
her on the beach for survey at Plymouth, the first comment
Father made was, " What a beautiful model " and " She ought
to sail well." I read years afterwards in the book " Immortal
Sails " that she had made the fastest passage of all the schooners
from Tremadoc Bay to Harbourg in Germany. My brief experience
of the *M. A. James* as a sailing schooner convinced me she was
a fast ship. For drawings of the *M. A. James* see Figures 1 and 2.
I think the reason this ship was misrepresented as slow was the
fault of those who sailed her. It is a definite fact that in sailing
a schooner, a man must have a thorough understanding of the set
of the tides and know when to hug the shore to get the first of the
tide in his favour and how to get the last of it. It is all a matter of
judgment and experience gained throughout the years of his life in
them and this cannot be done in a few months or years.

The man who has spent the greater part of his life in the deep
water trade is certainly at a great disadvantage when he attempts
to compete in a schooner on the coast, with those who have spent
all their lives coasting. I once heard a prominent citizen of my
home town in discussing the ability of a certain deep water man,
say, " My dear chap, this man holds a deep water master's
certificate, he's bound to know how to handle and work a coastal
schooner." In fact, very few of the schooner men held any
certificate at all, but in my time most of them knew their jobs
and if they were not capable of competing with others in the
same line of life they were very soon looking for a job. Even those
fortunate enough to own their own ship had to know their job to
keep going successfully. It was a separate and altogether different
life from a deep water life.

To come back to our Ilfracombe voyage, we beat up against
the strong wind and we found the *M. A. James* a fine ship and
powerful. We took in our gaff topsails but the upper topsail was
carried, and despite the pumping we carried on. One thing, of

course, was forcibly brought home to me. We had no competitors as far as sail was concerned, the old days were dead and gone but we three now sailing the *M. A. James* were in our own element. Even my brother so many years younger had sailed in a double topsail schooner for quite a long time. As I have said the braces had been stored for two years and were far from being good. The wind was bitterly cold and after four hours at the wheel, besides having to becket it every half hour to pump her out one was certainly glad to get below for a rest and, if possible, sleep.

One night off Trevose I had just got warm under the blankets in the middle watch when a shout came from Father, "Jump up, the fore brace has gone!" A new fore brace had to be roved off, and I had to do it. I hadn't been on a topsail yard for years and to keep it quiet I suggested backing the yards while I got the brace fitted, but Father overruled this and, as the coil of rope was waiting, I made fast the end round my waist and off I went up the rigging on the lee side. Now anyone who knows the job would understand it was not so easy to go out to the fore yard arm with the yard swinging about and in a heavy sea, especially the lee side. Being so very cold and pitch dark made it worse. When I got out, there was about two fathoms of fairly heavy chain, with a block on the end to pull up. This required both hands, so the rule of one hand for the ship and the other for yourself couldn't and didn't apply. I balanced across the end of the yard on my stomach as best I could and got it up, reeving the brace, bringing the end down with me, up the main rigging and fastened it. We braced her up again and then, of course, the water had gained so we pumped her out. When I got below again shivering with the cold it was going on for 2 a.m. so half my watch was gone and I was tired. It took me some time to doze off after the excitement and it seemed I had hardly closed my eyes, when my brother shouted eight bells so out I got for another four hours.

The next afternoon we were lying in the upper part of Bideford Bay with yards aback waiting for the first of the flood to make up round Morte and Baggy when an argument cropped up, through a chance remark of my brother's. He said, "Well we're coming to the end of the voyage and I must say I'm very glad. It's been pretty hard on me, with the vessel making water to have one watch to myself at night, while you two kept the other." I replied, red hot, "What are you talking about? I've had the watch to myself ever since we left!" Then Father stepped in and said. "You two suckers don't know the ropes yet. Of course you are both right." It came out at last that Father had told the same tale to both of us about being up all the time. He would certainly be on deck when I got up, and after George had gone below he'd say to me, "You know I can't trust that boy to handle the vessel like you blowing strong like this. I've got to be on deck with him so I'll go down below for an hour or two." Well up he'd come just before eight bells and say, "You go and make a cup of tea, I'll steer her." When George would come up, of course, he would see Father at the wheel. After having our cup of tea we would pump her dry and down I would go for my watch below. The *M. A. James* had a mess room fore side the cabin and I slept in a bunk there so that I wouldn't hear anyone going softly up or down the cabin and as soon as I had settled in, Father would be down below, leaving George to his watch alone. When the truth came out we looked at each other and laughed. After all Father was sixty-five and experience is a great teacher. You can see what Father looked like at this time from the photograph at Plate 19, which was taken on board the *M. A. James* at the end of this voyage. He is at the wheel, my brother George is next to him. The other person is one of my uncles. . . .

To return to the *Haldon*, after a number of voyages in her with the new motor I took on a contract to run coal from Ely Harbour to Padstow for a period of three months. It was a low freight, but we did two a week sometimes, if weather was fine, but again sometimes we were a fortnight on one. On the whole it was just a bare living.

It was while doing this work that I lost an eye through an accident. This was a severe blow to me. It happened in my own backyard. I had been sawing an old spar off and the saw wasn't very sharp. My brother tried to split a piece off the end with a hatchet, but not going far enough, I told him to drive it in with a hammer. A piece of steel came off the hatchet and into my right eye penetrating right through. I spent between two and three months in Exeter Eye Infirmary and had a tough time trying to save the eye, but eventually it had to be removed. It was financially hard too, as I had four boys in Bideford Grammar School and one in College, but I found I had good friends far away from my home. I had parcels of food and sweets from all over the west of England, and seeing the inmates at the infirmary in those days had to provide a lot of their own food, it was very acceptable. This provision of food was an understood thing and no fault could be found with the matron and staff, who all did their best for the patients under difficult circumstances, and lack of capital to provide full board. The infirmary was run on voluntary contributions with no State aid, and funds were low. I put on weight gaining over a stone and on the whole I think the enforced rest did me a lot of good.

About this time Father and Mother decided between them to give their children some of his money and, I feel, bearing in mind how he had valued his hard earned capital and saved it by sacrificing his own comfort, that the action he now contemplated was a very wonderful gesture. He gave every one of us £500 and seeing there were five sons and daughters it meant parting with £2,500. I cannot write all I would like to in appreciation. It came when I needed it most and it was the beginning of a closer bond than I had ever felt before. It wasn't so much the money but the different outlook and thought for his children that had prompted a man who set such a value on it to make a free gift.

I carried on for another year or so and one particular voyage caused not a little worry. I had discharged cement at Exeter and a cargo of barytes was offering for West Bank (Runcorn). As I have said, the *Haldon* was far from being a strong ship and barytes was a heavy cargo, but I made up my mind to risk it, hoping I wouldn't be caught in bad weather to strain her unduly. We got to Falmouth windbound, then a fine day appeared and we left in company with my cousin in the *Margaret Hobley*, also bound to Runcorn. The wind freshened westerly and she put her knight-heads under water more than a few times before we eventually rounded Land's End and squared away for the Smalls. I watched those pumps continually while we rolled and tumbled across the mouth of the Bristol Channel, expecting trouble, but she was tight as a drum. When we kept away to run up the St. George's Channel the wind died away and it became smooth. I thought, well, it's O.K. now, so I didn't bother to watch the pump as I had done previously.

When motoring up round the South Stack with a calm and smooth water I left the wheel to glance below at the engine. What I saw frightened me. The flywheel was in the water and doing nearly four hundred revolutions per minute, it was throwing the water up to the deck. I called all hands to man the pumps and we gradually gained on her, but we couldn't leave her longer than

fifteen minutes. All that day we took turns at the pumps and
when we anchored we were completely fagged out. My cousin
had anchored just before and seeing our trouble came on board
to help. They pumped while our tea was being prepared and in
the meantime I went below to stop the engine. Immediately the
noise of machinery stopped, I heard water gushing in somewhere
aft side of the engine. At first I thought of getting a bag of
sawdust to put under her, but listening carefully I pinpointed
the spot where I thought the leak would be. I got some tools
and cut out about two feet of the ceiling or inside plank and, sure
enough, there it was gushing up between the frames. The outside
seam of the plank had opened and there was no oakum in it for
a length of three or four inches, the water was simply pouring
in. I cut a piece of board to fit between the frames, put a plaster
of tar and oakum on it, thrusting it down on the inside of the
seam. I did not expect to stop it completely but to ease the rush
of water would be a great help, but I shored it down with wedges
and fastened it with nails. She was tight as a bottle again. We
discharged at West Bank, loaded in the same place for Plymouth
and when we came down to Newferry we grounded her on the
flats and I caulked that leak, so that there was no further trouble
with it. Several different ships had similar trouble in this way.
It was not due to weakness, but the waste lubricating oil would
get down there and rot the oakum. . . .

We continued in the Irish trade all next summer and in the
autumn got a contract from Ely Harbour, Cardiff, to Padstow.
That winter was a wild one and we didn't do very well, only
just keeping the wolf from the door. I earned very little cash
for myself. I left Appledore one morning with a south east wind
to try to get down to Padstow, but before we got to Hartland
the wind was south west and wild. We were forced back in over
Bideford Bar again. In the meantime a heavy ground sea had
come up. We caught it on the bar all right. A huge sea broke over
the stern. It unshipped the wheelhouse which also contained
the galley with stove, pots and pans, etc. The wheel was wrenched
out of its stands and I was under water pinned against the deck
house. The crew were in the rigging. They jumped down as
quickly as possible to release me, only just in time. We steered
her in by handling the wheelchains and finally moored in our
berth. Then we looked about, finding some of the galley utensils
and even the cast iron stove tops, right up in the bows under the

bowsprit. The damage was soon repaired, and I was glad when the winter was over. . . .

Among the skippers of auxiliary motor vessels belonging to Braunton and Appledore there was a sort of unwritten law, that if one ship broke down in a dangerous river such as the Severn, any other in company would immediately give assistance, and often one would tow the other a considerable distance. This was taken as a duty and no claim for salvage was ever made on the Braunton Shipowners Mutual Insurance Society of which Appledore ships were a considerable part. They may have had their differences and sometimes arguments would get heated, but the seafaring community of Braunton and Appledore never failed each other in time of need. It was the brotherhood of the sea which always came uppermost when required.

I remember on one occasion leaving Lydney in the early hours before daylight. It was very dark and our clutch refused to grip. We drifted a long way above the pier and all the others were gone down along, leaving us alone. I did my utmost to get the clutch right as there was a flat calm, but failed. Just as I had given up hope and made up my mind to get over to Hackthorn by sheering across with the anchor on the ground, I saw a high mast head light and two sidelamps coming towards us. This turned out to be the *Dido C.*, Captain Steve Chugg, and we were taken in tow. He had gone down with the others and when he missed us he came back searching and found us in difficulties. He towed us along for about two hours and when we got to the English and Welsh grounds light vessel our engine was ready. We had just started up when the *Dido C.* stopped. We were able to repay a little of our debt, but by far the greater debt of gratitude I still owe to the *Dido C.* and her owner Steve Chugg, a debt I shall never repay, but the great Architect of the universe no doubt remembered it when Steve died only a few years later.

Again in the Severn the *Millom Castle* broke down and I was some distance below when I saw her flag flying for assistance. Before I could get back to her she had gone down over the Counts, a dangerous reef of rocks, and the master had anchored. She had not touched, owing to high tides, but I was afraid to risk going down over them as tide was ebbing and it falls very fast in Severn. There is more water below the Counts than on top of them. I got the master to sheer across the tide towards the Innard Rocks and a little westerly wind helped her across. It was a lot of ebb when we finally got a rope on her and towed her down along. Going through the Shutes where I had formerly come to grief I found all the rocks, known as the Stones, above water. I towed the *Millom Castle* to the mud at Portishead and as I knew her engine would be right for the next tide I proceeded on my own leaving the *Millom Castle* in safety. I was too late on tide to tow her to Penarth and, in fact, we had some difficulty in getting there alone. She came down with us the following day and the first thing I heard was that I had run an enormous risk towing her through the Shutes so late on tide. This I disputed because as a boy with Father I could remember being off the Oares in the sailing ketch *Ulelia* and Father waiting for what he termed a fair tide through the " Shutes." It was considered safe to go through between Groggy and the Stones when the latter showed above water as the tide then set straight through. . . .

One Christmas we spent at Daunts Quay, Oyster Haven, and I think that was about the loneliest I ever remember. We were surrounded by wooded hills four or five times higher than our masts, blowing heavy gales at night, it was as if we had been dropped into a huge dark pit. On Christmas Eve I walked the four or five miles over fields and roads to the small town of Kinsale, bought a bag of food including Christmas fare and then walked back in the rain. That evening we sat in the cabin singing Christmas carols and trying to make each other happy. There was no habitation nearer than Kinsale. On Christmas morning I sat down and wrote a letter to my mother, filled it up with a lot of foolishness which set all the family laughing when they got it. I believe Mother still keeps that letter, she refuses to part with it. I was glad, a day or two later, to see some human beings come to start loading, and get out from between those depressing hills after we finished, but still it was good to be alive.

I've had many thrills of pleasure through my life and some setbacks, too, but in 1936 I had the pleasure of hearing my eldest son had obtained his B.A. degree, upper second, in English. I, of course, was too ambitious, I wanted a first class degree. He obliged me in this, too, for some years later he took Latin in his spare time as a schoolmaster and got an additional first class B.A. I have brought up a family of five boys to manhood, none of whom touched intoxicating liquor or smoked, but although they are temperate and all married, with their own children to rear, I wouldn't like to say they are all teetotal now. Of course, my wife

SAVE 35%

a quarter with a Direct Debit subscription

Subscribe to Amateur Photographer today by Direct Debit, the easiest and most convenient way to pay your subscription.

- **A subscription on Direct Debit** not only spreads the cost but saves you money too – pay only £13.26 a quarter.
- **Guaranteed home delivery every week,** with FREE postage and packing.
- Receiving Britain's biggest selling photographic weekly is the best way to keep up to date with all the latest developments.

Simply fill in the coupon below and let us do the rest.

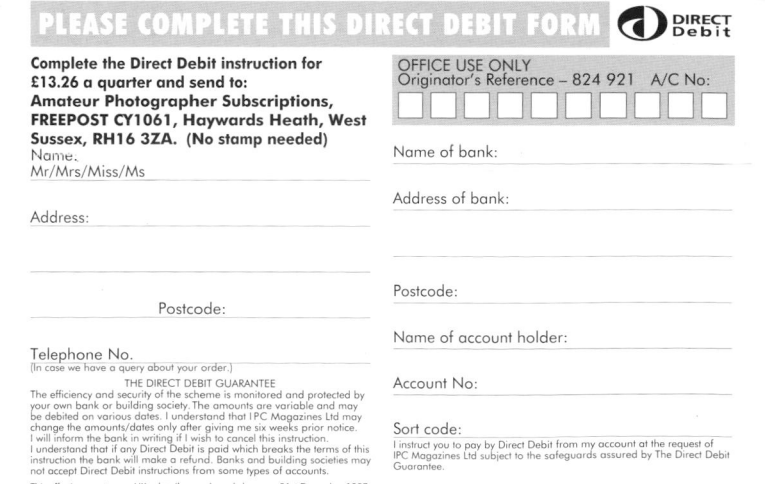

PLEASE COMPLETE THIS DIRECT DEBIT FORM

DIRECT Debit

Complete the Direct Debit instruction for £13.26 a quarter and send to:
Amateur Photographer Subscriptions, FREEPOST CY1061, Haywards Heath, West Sussex, RH16 3ZA. (No stamp needed)
Name.
Mr/Mrs/Miss/Ms

Address:

Postcode:

Telephone No.
(In case we have a query about your order.)

THE DIRECT DEBIT GUARANTEE
The efficiency and security of the scheme is monitored and protected by your own bank or building society. The amounts are variable and may be debited on various dates. I understand that IPC Magazines Ltd may change the amounts/dates only after giving me six weeks prior notice. I will inform the bank in writing if I wish to cancel this instruction.
I understand that if any Direct Debit is paid which breaks the terms of this instruction the bank will make a refund. Banks and building societies may not accept Direct Debit instructions from some types of accounts.

This offer is open to new UK subscribers only and closes on 31st December 1997. For enquiries and overseas orders please call: 01444 445555. Please allow up to 6 weeks for the delivery of your first subscription issue. The 35% discount is on the full price of £20.40 every quarter.

☐ Please tick this box if you prefer not to receive mailings from other companies.

OFFICE USE ONLY
Originator's Reference – 824 921   A/C No:

☐☐☐☐☐☐☐☐☐☐

Name of bank:

Address of bank:

Postcode:

Name of account holder:

Account No:

Sort code:
I instruct you to pay by Direct Debit from my account at the request of IPC Magazines Ltd subject to the safeguards assured by The Direct Debit Guarantee.

Signature:

Date:

Code: 20T

FIRST TEST Sigma's 100-300mm zoom – page 46

AMATEUR
PHOTOGRAPHER

FIRST WITH THE NEWS, VIEWS, TESTS AND PRICES EV

Expert tips for better bird photography
TECHNIQUE FILE

NEW SERIES
Small objects of desire

GALLERY
Bosnia in B&W

Spring colour

Focus on flowers & win big prizes

9 770002 684102

15>

SIMPLY RED
We test Kodak's new infrared slide film

SEE OVER FOR DETAILS

had all the responsibility of the family and whatever they are is her work.   Being always away myself I claim a very small share of credit, but I have a large share of pride in my wife's achievement.

My No. 2 son made a voyage with me after spending some time in an architect's office which was unfortunate for Ronald and myself as the principal to whom he was apprenticed died, leaving both of us very disappointed. On our way to Liverpool we had a very fine passage and Ron, of course was enthusiastic towards continuing in my footsteps.   I disagreed and told him if he wanted a seafaring career he must be apprenticed to a decent firm of shipowners and get a deep water certificate.   I could make no impression on him. His argument was that I had reared my family and he didn't see why he couldn't go and do likewise.   I explained our class of ship was dying out fast, but all my talk to him seemed futile.   I said nothing more but determined to show if the opportunity came that the life I led and that he seemed to want to follow was not a bed of roses, as it appeared on the voyage to Liverpool.

We discharged, loaded at Garston and sailed for home.   It blew very hard south west and we anchored in Redwharfe Bay for twenty-four hours.   Leaving there we tried to get to Holyhead, which we succeeded in doing after a struggle.   Ron was seasick and we washed all the pots and pans out of the galley during the performance.   Ron was still perky and one night after waiting for him late to come back on board, I made up my mind to sail and drive her home as hard as possible.   This was midnight on Thursday.   It was still blowing hard south west and one or two others of our class of ships remained at anchor.   We met plenty of sea and wind off the South Stack and had to reef down.   It was Sunday when we entered Fishguard Harbour and I was worn out having spent practically the whole time at the wheel.   Ron spent the time in his bunk very ill with seasickness and, I'm afraid, there was no shortage of salt sea water above and below. Entering Fishguard and now in smooth water, I called Ron up to help when sails and anchor were down.   I had to drag myself along to help stow the sails.   Ron saw I was worn out and said at once, " You sit down, Dad. I'll do the work now." We spent the remainder of Sunday quietly resting.   The next morning Ron and I pulled ashore, bought provisions, sent home, and then back on board to get under way again.   We had it bad enough until we got through the islands that night, but the following day

(Tuesday) we arrived home. Ron decided to give up the sea for good. Shortly after he became a police cadet.

But to return to our trading. We had blown away our mainsail on a voyage to Padstow and several of my friends considered our rig with a long poled mainmast as ideal for a Bermuda type mainsail. The pole from the eyes of the rigging up was approximately twenty-eight feet. I went home without a mainsail and got the sailmaker to make one to fit. I was dissatisfied from the first voyage. I found it utterly unsuitable for our ship, whereas before when loaded she would sail fairly well, now she was hopelessly inefficient, light and loaded. I had kept the main gaff until I found how this answered and now I made up my mind this would be the last jibheaded sail I would have. It should be borne in mind we still depended to a very large extent on sail.

We carried on doing the best we could for about twelve months and it was fortunate for me that we had no engine trouble. I had lost my mate through a little disagreement with his brother-in-law who sailed as able seaman with us, and being no business of mine I declined to interfere. We therefore carried on hoping the able seaman would soon be able to step up. He was a very hard worker, but not a fit person as yet to trust. However, I taught him the rule of the road at sea and whenever possible in difficult situations, would test him out until I was satisfied, and I put him mate, although he had a lot more to learn. It was getting very difficult to find a sailor and we had to do our best with what we could find. This threw a bigger strain than ever on the master, who had to be everything, Captain, Engineer, Able Seaman, Mate and Cook. In fact, life was getting unbearable for the master of our class of ship. Some were lucky to have good men, but if one lost them and had to carry on, it became often a nightmare.

Since the motor winch had come into the picture with our ships a lot of hard work in discharging of cargoes, setting sails and heaving anchors up, had been made a lot easier for the crew, and crews were reduced in number. Formerly, under sail alone, our ships such as *Donald & Doris*, *M. A. James*, *Margaret Hobley* and even the *Haldon* were considered as five handed, but now it was very rare to see them with more than three. It was the master who bore the brunt of the harder work, he was responsible for the maintenance of the machinery and had to put anything that went wrong in working order again. In our parents' days, in ships of this size, the master rarely worked cargo, unless, being by the share, he chose to save a man, when the amount saved went into his own pocket. In latter days, the master not only worked cargo with the crew, did the ship's business if and when he could spare the time, and looked after the engines, in most cases, where real sailors were scarce, he also had to maintain the ship and do such work as splicing rope and wire, repairing sails when necessary, and even going aloft to put up a ratline. I am not suggesting this was the case in every auxiliary sailing ship, but it was like this in the majority of cases. There were very few real sailors left, and the miracle ·was that we still kept the ships in fairly good condition, often through putting in long hours. When working cargo by winch, sometimes it would break down through a small part breaking. Then the hand winch had to be used and invariably it was the master and one other who went on the winch-handle. This was a rare occurrence, but if and when it happened, there was no other way out. . . .

After this there seemed little left for our ships but the Irish trade and this was nearly always a one-way traffic down to Ireland and back light to the Bristol Channel. There was an occasional cargo of scrap iron to bring back and, perhaps, a few potatoes. With freights very low, about five shillings to seven shillings per ton according to ports, it was difficult, sailing by the share, to get a living and I made many voyages for nothing. It was disheartening to work hard and have all the worry to find at the end of the return trip there was no remuneration. The ship needed her third of the freight to keep going. Luckily for my brother, cousins and myself, our parents knew all about our struggles. They got together and agreed that, for the time being, the ship's share should be one fourth instead of one third. This was cutting the ship to the bone. It couldn't go on; then the freights went up a little and immediately we agreed on paying one fourth plus one tenth. This worked all right until the war broke out when freights went up and the full third was again paid. The struggles of those years were often unbearable and I came to the conclusion the end was in sight for our ships. As they got lost or worn out they would never be replaced. The First World War had destroyed the best of them, no more were built and the sailors were becoming landsmen. The ships were scarce and not enough men to go round for those still trading. Wages were so low that men preferred to live on the dole, picking up a few shillings on the side or even sending their wives out to work for a few shillings.

I think the hardest period of the slump between the two world wars was between 1934 and 1938. The cut in freights to my mind was quite unnecessary and caused chaos everywhere among coastal shipowners. There were not enough cargoes to go round and this caused cut-throat competition of which merchants quickly took advantage. In their turn they had to cut everything to the bone. We were completely outclassed and driven from the coasts of Great Britain by the modern Dutch coaster, and only the Irish trade remained. There were too many ships for this individual trade which caused, not the healthy competition one hears of, but a most unhealthy one for the whole community. It temporarily ruined the little port of Appledore, where so many very fine wood ship's carpenters got their living and whose families were forced to live in extreme poverty. Wages in the dockyard fell to thirty-eight shillings and sixpence per week in Messrs. R. Cock & Son's yard, but to his lasting credit Mr. Fred Harris of P. K. Harris & Sons refused to cut lower than two pounds five shillings per week, stating that his men could not live on the money. Messrs. Cock went into liquidation and the lower dock was closed. Harris's kept going only with great difficulty and often took on work only to keep the yard open for the men.

On one occasion, for instance, the *Haldon* was lying off the yard with nothing to do, we had a few hard earned pounds in hand and in passing through the yard Father and I stopped to talk to Fred Harris. All our difficulties and troubles came up and Father said, " I have very little money in hand. I would like to stiffen up the *Haldon* with a couple of nine inch oak baulks but I never went in debt and I shall have to wait until she earns it." After a short conversation on the matter, Fred said, " I must keep the men in work and if you like I'll give you a price to see if we can arrange it." He went on board and that afternoon a contract was offered to put two nine inch oak baulks in each bilge, worked to the proper shape with through fastening in every other frame, four seams in the bilges outside port and starboard to be caulked and pitched and the knightheads, or rather bow chocks, in the vicinity to be raised up nine inches back to nothing at the fore rigging port and starboard with oak. The whole of the work was undertaken for the sum of thirty-six pounds nett. When we got that contract, Father said, " It's a dirt cheap job and we will accept it." The men were put on board the following morning and they were told the circumstances and asked to do

Plate 19.   *W. J. Slade*
  W. J. Slade's father, his brother George, and an uncle, on board the *M. A.*
James after she was brought home to Appledore. William Kingdon Slade was
65 years old when this photograph was taken.

Plate 20.   *National Maritime Museum*
There was always a crowd at the slip where the ferry from Instow landed.
The man with the bowler hat is probably " Daddy " Johns, one of the ferrymen.

their best. They did the work in quick time, I feel quite sure that Messrs. P. K. Harris & Sons made no profit whatsoever on the job, but as Fred Harris said, the yard remained open, and that was his main object. Today, both the yards are in a prosperous condition, all under the management of members of the Harris family, but it is people like ourselves who know what the people of Appledore owed to Fred Harris, who lived to see the yards prosper again before he died in 1951. . . .

I have already referred to the struggles of the years 1934 to 1938, before freights went up slightly, relieving the strain. We still kept our leg of mutton mizzen and mainsail but it didn't last much longer. We came up from an Irish port empty intending to load clay for the Mersey. When we got to Bideford Bay it was blowing hard westerly and we were under foresail, single reefed mainsail and single reef mizzen We hove to in Clovelly Roads to wait for tide in over the Bar and our engine started giving a bit of trouble through a pin in the plunger of the fuel pump breaking. It was about the size of an inch wire nail, so I got a nail in the hole to get us over the Bar. It was difficult to get in, with the plunger working, but with a little patience it could be done. I had a supply handy in case of need. I was below adjusting this when a heavy squall struck the ship. I jumped on deck and found the wind veering northerly, which meant we had to get out of Clovelly Roads. To set the mainsail properly the mast hoops secured the sail up to the eyes of the rigging, but there was thirty feet above that and that part of the sail was secured to a wire jack stay running from an eye bolt below the saddle of the mast right up to eyes of the topmast rigging The sail being reefed was down about five feet, and no one thought of losing the mast with a jib-headed sail, as there was no great strain with the sail reefed, but the unexpected happened in this case.

The eyebolt under the saddle broke, which threw a sudden heavy strain on the halyard, which went through a sheave hole in the top of the mast. The sudden jerk caused the mast to break seven feet above the eyas of main rigging. In a matter of seconds a piece of pitchpine spar about twenty feet long and nine or ten inches in the butt was flying around aloft hanging by wire stays. While we were trying to clear the wreckage the engine went wrong again, but we got the sail down without damage.

As we were now on a lee shore, having no ballast in and the mast gone, it became absolutely necessary to get the engine going

in order to prevent her driving ashore on Westward Ho! pebble
ridge, so I left the mate at the wheel to do his best, while I got
the engine going, if only at half speed. Things were getting
desperate and my crew were certainly not practical seamen. I
wanted to be everywhere at once. The mast had to take its chance
till I could get the engine going, which I did. We did not fetch
the bar buoy on the port tack and to try to get off was hopeless.
We came in over the tail about one hundred fathoms inside the bar
buoy. There was no ground swell and I reckoned to carry sufficient
water, it being now four hours flood. We kept away before the
wind when we got in the channel and when we passed Appledore
Quay I expected some assistance from the hoveller I usually
employed, but it was Sunday and no one came. We anchored
on Newquay Ridge, off Harris's yard, with two anchors. It was
blowing a gale almost, and I had to get the wreckage down before
the fore and aft foresail would come down. It took me about
four hours, but at last it was all secured and I had done enough
to make me completely worn out. I got ashore just before the
ship ebbed dry.

When I got to my father's house in Appledore he enquired
where the vessel was. I replied, " On the ridge with the mainmast gone." The family had been to church and owing to the
wild weather, had not gone along the Quay, so they did not know
of our accident. It had puzzled me why I had not had some help,
but, of course, Father didn't know and no one told him.

The following morning we shifted to a berth alongside the
ship-carpenter's yard. After examination, we found an ordinary
cap could easily be fitted on the top of the broken mast, a topmast sent up in the usual way, so that instead of having a pole
mast, it would have the usual doublings and cross trees. We had
a topmast belonging to one of the other ships and a pair of cross
trees, so we set about rigging a stage around the mast head for
a carpenter to go aloft to fit the cap. This was only a few hours'
work, so that we were soon ready to load our cargo. The worst
job was altering the mainsail to a gaff sail again. We took on
board our old gaff and soon found the required number of blocks
for the main and peak halyards. For the gaff topsail we put a
spare staysail up, and I myself altered it to fit. On the whole I
didn't regret carrying that mast away and re-rigging the ship
with gaff sails and topsails. We had carried away the pole of the
foremast off the Lizard some time before. It broke off in a knot,

again above the top peak halyard block. I think the *Haldon* was the first ship rigged at Appledore in this way as a fore and aft schooner with fore and main gaff topsails, the *Maud Mary* followed and later the *Kathleen & May* was very similar. The two latter ships never had a leg of mutton mainsail and I think they are wise to retain the gaff sails. Some time later I also condemned the mizzen and replaced it with a gaff sail. I had certainly learned a lesson, but I suppose when the ships started to have more powerful motors, making them practically full powered, it wouldn't matter so much, especially when they were only going on short trips in the Bristol Channel.

We struggled along for another twelve months in the usual way hoping for an improvement which did not materialise, but the strain of bringing the family up had eased. My eldest son was well established as a Grammar School master, the second son doing well in the police force, the third son in an auctioneer's office and my fourth as a clerk in Lloyds bank. Only one remained and he was still in Bideford Grammar School.

Then came another catastrophe. I had discharged scrap in Port Talbot and as usual found difficulty in getting a freight. Everyone who knows this port will realise it is a long walk from the lock gates to the town and during the last day there, I had walked the length of the docks to answer telegrams several times. Finally, I chartered to load clay at Bideford for the Mersey. We sailed in the evening for home and it was dark when we got clear of Port Talbot. I remained at the wheel until well outside the Scarweather Lightship, and the weather being fine with a moderate breeze northwest, I suggested we should have our supper, after which I would sit down in our little cabin to rest my feet. It is only a few steps to the wheel from the cabin where I sat. The crew had their supper and I was relieved to have mine.

After I had finished, I sat there a short time looking at my papers and accounts. Altogether I had been off the deck about half an hour, when I heard the mate shout, " Oh ! my God ! " Realising something was wrong I jumped for the deck, reached the wheel as we struck a light oil tanker stem on into her port side. The crew were taking to the boat without bothering where I was. I yelled to them to stop lowering the boat, while I steered our ship clear of the other. When I went forward to ascertain the extent of the damage, I got a shock. She was completely shattered down to the light water mark. If she had been loaded, there is

no doubt she would have sunk like a stone. I entered the forecastle
and found water rushing in but no more than we could cope with.
The mate suggested we let her sink and take to the boat, but I
couldn't do that without a struggle to save her, so made up my
mind to risk getting her home. If the slightest bit of sea got up
she was bound to sink, but it looked fine. On questioning the
crew they told the same yarn about the steamer coming up behind
and suddenly crossing our bow. I couldn't understand it and
felt there was something being kept back. I tried them all ways
to get something else, but they still stuck to the same tale. We
got across into Bideford Bay and in the morning moored at
Appledore. . . .

It now became plain that, being so badly damaged, we should
have to throw the ship on the Braunton Insurance Club for
survey, but as no one could decide, it was agreed that a surveyor
from the Sailing Ship Mutual Insurance of London should survey
without prejudice. Two qualified men attended and a figure
was agreed between them of seven hundred and sixty pounds.
Now I had always acted for my father in his dealing with the
club as a member of its committee and in consequence I had
acquired a thorough knowledge of its functions and, in fact, there
was little anyone could tell me about it. I got a statement in
writing from the surveyors and on the strength of this claimed
my insurance.

To have a proper outlook on this matter, it is, perhaps, necessary
to explain how our insurance was worked. The Braunton Club
was only for Total Loss and/or Constructive Total Loss and
Salvage. The club enrolled in the Sailing Ship Mutual
Insurance Association and they undertook to fight law cases,
pay for damage done to others, and give protection in various
ways, such as recovery of freight, compensation, etc. The Total
Loss & C.T.L. was entirely on the Braunton Club. If the ship
damaged herself the owner paid for it. Now, in the case of our
collision it was evident that, despite what the crew said, the
Haldon was entirely to blame and, therefore, the owner paid for
his own repairs, but a clause in the policy stated, if the damage
exceeded fifty per cent. of the total value as agreed by the club,
she became a " Constructive Total Loss " and, therefore, entitled
to claim insurance. A clause limiting this amount barred the
owner from being fully insured, i.e., if a ship was valued by the
club at one thousand pounds, the amount of insurance allowed

from all sources could not exceed five hundred pounds or half value. The owner was compelled to accept the risk in Total Loss or C.T.L. of half the ship's value. For this, each ship paid three pounds per cent. per annum on the half value insured. Similarly, in case of salvage the owner paid one half and the Braunton Club the other half.

The *Haldon* was valued for insurance purposes in one thousand two hundred pounds and insured for six hundred pounds. As the estimate of damage was seven hundred and sixty pounds, which was more than fifty per cent. of the total value, I was entitled to six hundred pounds insurance less seven pounds ten shillings owing in premium. In course of time I therefore received five hundred and ninety two pounds ten shillings from the Braunton Shipowners Mutual Insurance Association Ltd.

The ship now theoretically became the property of the club. When I asked what they intended to do with her, I was told to take her upon the mud and let her rot. To this I objected pointing out that according to their policy the ship should be sold by auction to the highest bidder and the proceeds, less expenses, shared equally between the owner and the club. A meeting of the committee was held, and it was considered by them she was not worth putting up for auction as it would be all swallowed up in expenses. I offered eighty pounds as she stood and the club asked for one hundred pounds. We compromised and I agreed to ninety pounds, sending a cheque for forty-five pounds and retaining my half, forty-five pounds, to which I was entitled.

I had tried to buy another ship but failed to get a suitable one. I therefore determined to repair the *Haldon* as the cheapest way out. We were fortunate to be able to get a large quantity of splendid secondhand wood, African mahogany, for repairs and also a secondhand bowsprit. This was a great help towards the cost of repairs but even with this help and all the work we ourselves did, the cost of repairs was considerably in excess of the amount I received in insurance. When the *Haldon* came out of dock she was a much better ship than before Her old knight-heads were found to have been broken years before and now she was practically rebuilt forward.

I came out of dry dock and away from Appledore with a fresh mate, who had formerly been master in schooners and ketches. I was, therefore, able to have a comfortable watch below when weather was moderate.

H

CHAPTER 6

THE SECOND WORLD WAR AND THE END
OF IT ALL

WE CARRIED ON in the Irish trade for some time. With the exception of one third of the ship owned by my cousin in Cardiff, the *Haldon* belonged to me, and I was now doing very well with a rise in freights. We made several voyages to Ireland and then the Second World War broke out. During the phoney period it made little or no difference to us, but when the minefield was laid across the St. George's Channel, some of the ships saw difficulties ahead and didn't care about going up by the Tusker and down close to shore as they now had to do to reach Ireland. It wasn't so bad in summer but when winter started to set in, it was a difficult route for what was practically a sailing vessel. The freights, of course, jumped up to double and soon it became a paying business all through.

When the minefield was first laid I was home with my ship. I went to Appledore where I met my father, he tried to persuade me to stay home and lay the ship up. He did his best, but I told him the authorities could not block the channel altogether and I was certain there would be a route laid down to follow.

Only one thing marred our home life and that was Father's failing health. He was going downhill fast, but he refused to give up, insisting on his gardening being done. Some time previous to this, he had given away the second two thousand five hundred pounds to his children, but, of course, he made provision for Mother, so there was nothing to worry about on that score. He liked to walk up through the shipyard to see the vessels, but he took no active part in the working of them.

With Christmas over, we started again in the Irish trade and got quite used to the Tusker route. All the bar vessels were generally together. On one particular voyage, just prior to the minefield being laid, four or five including the *M. A. James*, the schooner *Kathleen & May*, the *Margaret Hobley*, the ketches *Bessie Ellen* and *Progress*, with, of course, ourselves in the *Haldon*, left Penarth Dock with a south east wind. We were left behind, as usual. They were soon out of sight, but when I passed St. Govens Lightship I could see several lots of sidelamps in under the land. The wind was freshening and looked very dirty. I did not go in towards those lights as I guessed some were hanging on to go into Milford. It seemed an awful time to wait from 2 a.m. to 9 a.m. They were not allowed to enter before, owing to wartime restrictions. I thought about the tide in our favour and the distance to Waterford Harbour with daylight coming on and I decided to risk it. We got outside the Smalls and it was now blowing hard southerly. We reefed her down and ran for Waterford intending to make the land just below the entrance. There was plenty of heavy sea water on board, but we remained inside the wheelhouse and shut the doors. None of us got wet and even our feet were dry. We were getting well over to the Irish side at 8 a.m. and being very dirty we kept a sharp lookout for land. Suddenly I picked it up and, knowing we were below, jibed over. We were only about one mile off and the flood tide now going into Waterford Harbour. In a short time I saw the piers of Dunmore East and went right in to anchor at Passage East. The customs boarded us, he only stayed a few minutes. I gave him a telegram to send home. Father was worried about the *M. A. James* but they were not allowed into Milford till 10 a.m., so I had done the right thing this time. On our way back light we saw the others coming out of Milford. . . .

Shortly afterwards my mate decided he had seen enough of the Irish trade and again I was without a trustworthy man to leave on deck. The situation was steadily getting worse. Freights were good, but it was almost impossible to get a good sailor who knew his job, and, although it was now profitable, life for the master in one of these ships was certainly very far from being a bed of roses. Those who had reasonably good crews were indeed lucky, but we had to do our best to keep running. I got an Appledore man to go, he was a good worker, but knew very little about going to sea. However, any man brought up among boats and barges in Appledore soon learns to make himself useful, so we managed to carry on in the Irish trade, although it wasn't exactly comfortable to have to run up to the Tusker in winter with an empty ship and then across to the Bristol Channel. There was always the chance of a westerly wind backing southerly and catching us to leeward, unable to weather up in Milford, in which case, our prospects were not inviting.

One voyage we loaded scrap iron at Dungarvon for Briton Ferry. As usual we proceeded to the Tusker and across. Now the wind being easterly we steered for the South Bishop off the Pembroke coast. Just before dark it became very thick and dirty and I, being anxious to make the Bishops before dark, left the wheel, and walked to the lee rail to look ahead. I was only about six to eight feet from the wheel, but what I saw just under the bow made me jump that six feet, grab the wheel and heave it to port. Just in time a floating mine, presumably one of our own, broken adrift, passed along the lee quarter, only a few feet away. I think I must have been born under a lucky star. Had we struck that mine, I suppose we should have been blown out of the water in bits. I reported this on arrival, but by this time, it was a common occurrence and mines often floated ashore. Just after we passed this, our engine stopped without warning and I immediately heard the fog signal on the Bishops. We started up at once and very soon after, passed up Milford, and so to our destination without further excitement or worry. From now on we got quite a lot of short trips within the Bristol Channel limits, but did not quite neglect our Irish friends.

I was discharging in Glandore in the County of Cork one particular voyage when I got a telegram relayed from my father at Appledore. It stated, " Haldon requisitioned by H.M. Government for balloon barrage purposes, proceed to Appledore for inspection." I was chartered to go to Lydney to load a cargo for Glandore again at a rate of freight I had only dreamed of for many years and after having had such a struggle I resented the idea of losing an obvious chance to make a bit of money. For the life of me, I couldn't see the necessity of taking all our ships away from us. I don't know how the idea originated, but I still feel it was not a good one and eventually it did incalculable damage to all the small shipowners of Braunton and Appledore from which we never recovered. Those remaining in the trade had no opposition and did well financially, but the owners of the ships that were requisitioned had a very raw deal, being paid a miserable pittance by the Government on a pre-war scale of freight and in the end the ships were sent back to the owners as total wrecks through sheer wanton neglect or lack of understanding and knowledge of a wood ship.

But to return to the *Haldon*. It didn't take me long to see my way out of that difficulty. On looking again at the telegram I found it had been sent to my father who, of course, was W. Slade, but W. Slade of " Haldon," Myrtle Street, Appledore, was not the owner of the schooner *Haldon* and, further, he had not owned anything in her for years. I was the owner and my address was Bideford. I made up my mind to have a last fling before being caught, so ignored that telegram altogether and proceeded to Lydney to fulfil my charter. When we were loaded, being neap tides I was able to go home for a week-end. There I found all the requisitioned ships about to be surveyed, and most of them hoping for release. I had to have some conversation with the officer attached to the Admiralty for the taking over of these craft, really about the *M. A. James*, but during this talk he asked where the *Haldon* was lying and I replied she is at Lydney and I am her master. He said, " You were ordered to Appledore for survey." I replied : " Did you send me a requisition telegram ? " He looked up his list and sure enough it was there, addressed to W. Slade, " Haldon," Appledore—Devon. " Well," I said, " I'm afraid you've blundered in my case. I'm the owner of the *Haldon* and she has nothing to do with the man you sent to. I'm W. Slade but my home is in Bideford." After some argument I and my ship were rejected. The rest were all taken except the *Kathleen & May* and the *Emma Louise*.

For my own part, I was delighted to have gained my freedom to live and, in my opinion, instead of taking these badly needed coastal trading ships, plenty of other means could have been found to do the job of supporting balloons at a saving of tens of thousands of pounds of the taxpayers' money. There were men put in as overseers on our ships who had no idea of what was necessary to keep them in proper condition. The men who were the former masters of the schooners, who knew their jobs, were not allowed to have any voice in their upkeep, and indeed were often treated as ignoramuses. . . .

To get back to the *Haldon*, we continued on our usual routes of Bristol Channel short trips and an occasional Irish voyage. I think one episode well worth mentioning, although it did not directly concern me. I have mentioned the difficulties with

regard to getting crews and most of our vessels carried anyone
they could get hold of in the small Irish ports.   Well, this case
concerns the one hundred and twenty tons ketch *Garlandstone*. Her
master and owner at this time was a man in his sixties who was
a native of one of the villages on Gloucester Canal.   I think it was
either Saul or Arlingham.   I refer to that grand old sailor, Andrew
Murdock, well known to all West Country sailors.   He found
himself at Courtmacsherry without a crew but it didn't worry
Andrew, he got some men to come on board to set sails with him,
cast off the moorings and sailed alone.   He went direct for the
Bristol Channel up over all the minefield.   When he felt tired he
hove her to and turned in to sleep.   Finally he got to Kingroad,
spoke to the Gloucester tug asking them to tell Lydney harbour-
master he was coming up the Severn to Lydney on his own with
no crew and to have one of the dock head men ready to jump
on board to put a rope ashore when he put her alongside the pier.
Everything went as planned and he arrived in the canal without
any mishap.   I don't know whether he ever took the *Garlandstone*
to sea again but even if not I would like to feel as good at that
age as he was.

I did, eventually, come up over the minefield direct from the
Old Head of Kinsale to Lundy on several occasions and I must
confess to feeling very relieved when I knew we were all clear of it.
Andrew Murdock was alone, he was a much older man than I
and he was the first of the Irish traders to risk it.   We were all
warned to keep clear, so I suppose there was considerable risk,
especially when a heavy sea with a strong wind had come up,
as it did on one of our trips over it.   I never heard how deep those
mines were moored, but a good number broke adrift and washed
ashore on the coasts of Ireland and West of England, proving at
least that this minefield did exist. . . .

Shortly after this I found my sight was suffering and the
knocking about I had received in an air raid at Avonmouth,
coupled with entering and leaving harbours in the dark, hadn't
helped my one eye, and I was definitely feeling the strain on it.
Sometimes I felt like giving up, but then the urge would come to
go again.   Apart from our regular Christmas breaks I had never
been ashore for a holiday and never out of a berth, with the
exception of one week in 1917 when I had lost the *W. D. Potts*
under shell fire, and two months in hospital after losing my right
eye.   During the week after losing the *W. D. Potts* I was trawling

in Bideford Bay so that could hardly be called a holiday. To be continually at work in the coasting trade for thirty-nine years was not a bad record, especially when it is considered I had to cope with the business part of running the ships as well as working cargoes whenever possible. Sometimes I longed to be able to go to some remote place so that I would never even hear about the ships and thus rest my brain and body, but that didn't come until several years later.

One of my last voyages in the *Haldon*, a very short one, taught me a lesson I had yet to learn and that was that I could get into serious trouble even in the Bristol Channel. I had loaded a light cargo of barley for Swansea and got to Penarth mud where I was windbound for several days. It irritated me to be windbound on such a short trip, so I left thinking how ridiculous it was to wait for moderate weather to do that contemptible little journey. When we got below Barry, the wind freshened to a south south east point and we had to double reef down. Now Swansea Bay in a strong south south east wind is not a very pleasant spot for a small auxiliary sailing vessel. It came on very dirty which didn't help matters and, being lightly loaded, she needed her engine to handle her in narrow waters. We got inside the Mumble Head all right, reached into comparatively smooth water by the passenger pier in order to get the signals for entering. We hove around on the starboard tack heading off, but the patrol boat steamed away without hailing us at all. The engine chose this moment to give out, although it had been A1 for some considerable time. One of those confounded pins in the fuel pump had broken again, but I was now in a very awkward position. Among the big deepwater ships anchored there I couldn't leave the wheel and neither of the crew could put the engine right. Being so dirty I lost the Mumble Head. The vessel towing her three-bladed propellor refused to stay or wear. She wore off before the wind but refused to go far enough to jibe over, she was just running ashore pretty fast and I knew she was heading too far up the bay for Swansea. The wheel was useless to her. I lowered away the main peak halyards, she gradually went off and jibbed, but by this time I judged her too far up to the eastward. I could see nothing in the thick rain, so set the mainsail again to drive her down on the port tack. Then we saw the outer buoy off Swansea piers close to leeward. I had to get her before the wind quickly. I yelled, " Lower down the mainsail ! " and my crew promptly started lowering the foresail. I yelled again and they stopped. In the meantime, I had hove the wheel hard up and jumped to the mainsail myself. I let it run and she went off heading for the piers at low water. Owing to the force of the weather we carried water right up to the North Dock while my crew struggled to get the sails down. They never succeeded so I stuck her against the mud bank so that I could go with them. We got the sails stowed and I soon had the engine in order. We got in dock that evening and I never felt more relieved. So much for being caught in a difficult position with a poor crew. It simply meant that I could not afford to run the risk of being out in bad weather unless I could get a good man with me, and these were, indeed, hard to find.

Later on I got a good man out of the balloon barrage service, W. Cox, who had been master of his father's ship, the *Welcome*, and was delighted to sail with me as mate. We left home now well-manned for Swansea to load patent fuel for Sharpness. When we arrived to Sharpness I rang up the agent and he told me I could go home for the week-end. This was Saturday morning, so home I went. After I had left, the cargo was out and a message came that the vessel could load oats for Barry. W. Cox answered the phone and chartered the vessel in my name. He loaded her on the Sunday and I left for Sharpness on the Monday morning before post came. When I got to Sharpness I was told the vessel had left that morning for either Cardiff or Barry. I went to Cardiff by rail just in time to catch the agent who then told me to go to Barry, where I found her waiting to discharge. Of course, there was a good laugh about it, but I began to feel I could afford to let Bill run the vessel while I stayed home to do the business part.

We continued in the Bristol Channel trade for a few more months and I had a very easy time. We loaded a cargo of wheat for Swansea and this was my last cargo to that port. We had anchored off the passenger pier, inside the Mumble Head with a strong southerly wind. We had to go into Swansea about 3 a.m. It was black dark and dirty weather. We got inside and up to the South Dock all right, but I really couldn't see where I was going. There were no lights and I was just guessing where the North Dock pier was. Then Bill came and asked if I saw the pier and I replied, " No." He pointed it out but still it was just a black wall to me. I couldn't see it. He offered to take the wheel, but I felt this was giving up my job and I refused. We got alongside all right, but I realised at last that in these conditions my sight was not equal to the job and it was time I got out. We loaded in Swansea for Bideford. I thought a lot about it and finally asked Bill if he would like to take charge of the *Haldon*. He was, of course, very pleased and so in September, 1943, I gave up my berth as master to a younger and much fitter man.

In the meantime, my father had passed to his final account, so there was plenty for me to do. I had the *Haldon* and the requisitioned *M. A. James* to manage, in addition to which I went fishing. I certainly did not give up work, nor did I give up my connection with the sea. Until the armistice was signed I did my share of watch keeping at night in civil defence work without losing a tide at fishing.

I found plenty of work to do as the months rolled on, there was always some business in reference to the ships and cash was coming along in sufficient amounts to keep me going. Then came the end of the war and the return of our ships from balloon barrage service and the appointment of watchmen. They came in over the Bar under their own power for the most part but one or two had to be towed in. They were all moored off Appledore Dockyards ready for survey and I was one of the longshore sailors appointed to watch at four pounds four shillings per week, day time only. It wasn't long before they had to be unmoored or shifted around and I pointed out to the agent that we were watchmen and to be up all hours, shifting the craft was not part of a watchman's job. So other arrangements were then made for men to do the shifting and sometimes we came into our share of this.

The *Donald & Doris* was the first to go in dock for survey and naturally I took a great interest with my cousin in the outcome of these proceedings. The ballast was taken out and during survey it was found the ship had been so badly neglected that her keel, stem and sternpost were eaten away with mussels and her planking badly wormed. She had been strained through carelessness in laying her badly when being kept on the beach. In fact, the task of repairing, unless paid for by the Government, was not practicable. The estimate for repairs, which, of course, was only an estimate and in no way binding, was between three thousand five hundred and four thousand pounds. It was the duty of the authorities to put those ships back in the same condition as when they took them, but this was ignored as they considered they were C.T.L. (Constructive Total Loss).

There were prolonged negotiations with the Government over

our compensation for these ruined ships. Finally it was agreed
that they would pay four thousand pounds for the *M. A. James*
and the wreck would be my property to dispose of as I wished.
I approached Mr. Harris about repairs, but deterioration had
played havoc with the ships and I was told there would be no
change out of five thousand pounds to repair the *M. A. James*. As
we had not earned the money this was impossible. It was one
thousand over her market value and we decided it was, indeed, a
Constructive Total Loss. I subsequently sold the wreck for seven
hundred pounds including the engine to Mr. Percy Harris. They
decided against repairs and resold the engine to Gloucester. The
ship played a part in lifting an eighty-ton crane that had fallen in
the river from Harris's yard and was then totally finished. The
remains of the *M. A. James* still lie in the river above Appledore.
The end of one of the finest and best built schooners that had sailed
the Atlantic Ocean and the Mediterranean for many years. It
was a shame to see her go like this but all good things come to an
end and she was a real good thing ruined by the incompetence
and folly of irresponsible men.

While all this had been going on I had disposed of the *Haldon*.
We had bought her in 1923 for one thousand two hundred pounds.
I sold her in 1944 for two thousand five hundred pounds. She
was always a trouble but I earned a good living in her and sold
her at a profit. I had no regrets.

After the war finished a large number of landing craft came
to Appledore to lay up and I earned quite a few pounds in looking
after some of these. There was always something to do to their
mooring or pumping them out. I was continually employed while
they stayed in Appledore and when the end of them came I thought
I was finished but there were still jobs for me to do afloat. I went
away to bring home different craft and took some away. I also
did quite a lot of surveying wooden craft which kept my mind
occupied.

When the landing barges went I turned my spare time to good
account by building model schooners and ketches. I was in the
habit of spending a lot of time watching the mine sweepers being
built of wood at Messrs. P. K. Harris & Son's yard and then the
planks being fitted. I came to the conclusion I could do the job.
I bought the plans of a Brixham trawler first. I built her from
those plans, every frame in its proper place. When she was rigged
I sailed the finished article in Bideford River and she *would* sail

too, beautifully, with a curl of foam climbing up over her stem. My next model was the barquentine *Waterwitch*. Then came a model of *M. A. James* rigged as a double topsail and standing top-gallant yard schooner. This was sailed by putting ballast in the hold and she was also quite good. I sold her very profitably indeed.

I soon replaced that model with one of an Appledore built schooner called the *Katie*. The original of this model was a lovely little ship painted white. She was built by R. Cock & Sons for a Captain Griffiths of Portmadoc. She sailed all over the Atlantic and to Mediterranean ports and was finally lost in the West Indies through striking a reef. One of Appledore's old coasting skippers sailed as mate in her for years, he had only one hand and a steel hook, but it was wonderful what he could do with that hook from skinning potatoes to splicing wire. He was one of Appledore's finest sailors and was in the *Katie* when she was lost. He was very pleased with the model and considered it was a good representation of the ship, including the cut of her sails. Since this I have managed to do one or two others, our ketch *Ulelia*, the *W. D. Potts*, and finally, the *Millom Castle*, and have managed to improve the standard each time I try another. . . .

Well, now I feel it is time I closed this rather rough and, perhaps, garbled account of the life of a coastal sailor. Sometimes it was hard to endure and, of course, in summertime it was often a pleasure. There were times when life became almost intolerable, but compensation for this could always be found. It took us away from home for long periods, often months, but seafaring men learned to appreciate the saying that "Absence makes the heart grow fonder" more than the average person. If I were asked the question: "Do you regret your life on the sea?" I would, after careful thought, say, "To be born as I was in a seafaring community of a seafaring family, in those days, there was nothing better I could have done." For practically forty years I was seasick, but during all the years of my manhood I never allowed this to get me down. I was always ready to face another bout of this miserable affliction. I wonder sometimes if it wasn't really a blessing in disguise. Although getting on in years I have yet to face the first illness due, perhaps, to having my system cleared of its impurities. I have often regretted my inability to get away to a deepwater life. Yes, I think I would have gone to the top in that sphere of life and probably spent many years as master in a

deepwater ship, but would this have been a more remunerative
or comfortable existence? I have great doubts. For one thing
I was my own master for the big majority of those years at sea,
responsible to no one, a freedom that could not exist in any other
branch of sea life. Now I can sit back and with my seafaring
friends recall my experiences and, perhaps, live over again some
of life's pleasures and watch my sons' progress, enjoying their
successes, and ready as always to step in to help, if and when
troubles come along for them.

Yes, both my wife and I are proud to have reared a family
who are good citizens and can be trusted to keep themselves
respected by the community among whom they live.

I have written this account at the earnest request of my friends,
Basil Greenhill, author of " Merchant Schooners " and Commander
H. Oliver Hill of the National Maritime Museum.

I sincerely hope it will meet with their approval.

Bideford, 1954-1957.   W. J. SLADE

APPENDIX 1

LIST OF THE VESSELS OWNED BY THE SLADE FAMILY OF APPLEDORE

1888-1948

Compiled by H. Oliver Hill

Number	Name	Main Port of Registration	Rig	Where built	When built	Tons	Dimensions	Period owned by Slade Family
69503	Nouvelle Marie	Bideford	Ketch	France	1869	49	Not known	1888-1909

Notes on History: *First appears in British Register 1879. Owned by William Nolan, Shirken Island, County Cork, sold by him to Mrs. Mary Ann Quance in 1888. Originally a two-masted schooner, later a ketch. Ran back to Bristol Channel in south west gale when bound for Bude with coal from Newport, and was lost with all hands on the Chapel Rock off Barry, March 25th, 1909.*

Number	Name	Main Port of Registration	Rig	Where built	When built	Tons	Dimensions	Period owned by Slade Family
62974	Heather Bell	Bideford	Ketch	Barnstaple	1870	53	72.0 x 9.5 x 8.8	1896-1922

Notes on History: *Launched as a schooner and first registered at Bridgwater under ownership of J. Allen of Watchet. Converted to ketch rig in 1893. Sold in 1882 to owners in Isle of Man. Lost at Coverack in 1922 in circumstances described in Chapter 4 of this book.*

Number	Name	Main Port of Registration	Rig	Where built	When built	Tons	Dimensions	Period owned by Slade Family
63504	Alpha	Bideford	Ketch	Truro	1871	60	72.2 × 19.3 × 8.8	1897-1912

Notes on History: *Built as a fore and aft schooner for C. B. Kelway of Truro, who ran her in the North Atlantic trade to Newfoundland. In 1884 she was owned by William Penrose of Truro and from 1885-1888 by John Estlick of Truro. From 1888-1897 she was owned by Joseph W. Hunkin of Truro. In 1912 W. K. Slade sold her to John Cox of Appledore, a relative of the W. Cox who took over the "Haldon" when W. J. Slade retired. An auxiliary motor of 22 h.p. was installed in 1924 and the vessel was lost in Bideford Bay in 1933.*

Number	Name	Main Port of Registration	Rig	Where built	When built	Tons	Dimensions	Period owned by Slade Family
74429	Ulelia	Truro	Ketch	Truro	1877	58	75.4 x 19.9 x 9.4	1899-1916

Notes on History: *Built as a fore and aft schooner for North Atlantic trade to Newfoundland in which business she was owned successively by John Estlick, and Gavin McF. Hope. She ran out of class and was bought by William Drake of Braunton for the coastal trade and run as a fore and aft schooner for a year until she was bought by George Quance and W. K. Slade on a 50-50 basis. George Quance drafted her rig as a ketch and rerigged her. Like the "Alpha" she had a beautiful hull and though she had not been outstanding as a schooner she proved very fast as a ketch. She was sold in 1916 and was owned in Appledore successively by Mrs. Taylor, Mrs. Hobbs, John Hutchings and Percy Harris. She was lost on the rocks when entering Rhoscarberry, Ireland, as a result of missing stays, in 1930.*

Number	Name	Main Port of Registration	Rig	Where built	When built	Tons	Dimensions	Period owned by Slade Family
68283	Fanny	Plymouth	Ketch	Feock	1872	53	62.2 x 17.0 x 7.1	1898-1907

Notes on History: *Built by Scobie at Malpas and first owned by Richard Skinner Hitchins of Truro. Owned in Plymouth from 1883 to 1898 by William Sarah, Joseph Ellis and William David Crooks in turn. Stranded under Lizard, July 23rd, 1907, when bound for Lydney in ballast from Cadgwith, all hands saved.*

Number	Name	Main Port of Registration	Rig	Where built	When built	Tons	Dimensions	Period owned by Slade Family
16935	Bristol Packet	Newport	Smack	Newport	1857	53	Not known	1899-1902

Notes on History: *Owned in Newport from 1858 to 1877 she was sold to Cork in the latter year and back to Cardiff in 1889. She was bought by G. R. Kirsey of Appledore in 1897 and subsequently owned by Joseph Evans, W. J. Lord and Thomas Fishwick as well as by James Slade. She was condemned after damage at Porth Luney Cove, Cornwall, and broken up in March, 1916. Photographs show her to have been rigged as a ketch in her later years.*

Number	Name	Rig	Main Port of Registration	Where built	When built	Tons	Dimensions	Period owned by Slade Family
79131	Lewisman	Ketch	Bideford	Stornoway	1878	58	90.1 × 18.1 × 8.1	1901-1927

Notes on History: *Built as a schooner and owned in Scotland until 1884. Bought by William Sarah of Plymouth, converted to ketch rig in 1889 and sold to William Holden of Oreston in 1895. An auxiliary motor of 30 h.p. was fitted in 1927 in which year she was sold to Sidney W. Slater of Barnstaple. She was sold back to Scotland and registered at Leith after the Second World War. She does not appear in 1955 Mercantile Navy list and at the time this book was written was probably lying worn out in a Scottish creek.*

Number	Name	Rig	Main Port of Registration	Where built	When built	Tons	Dimensions	Period owned by Slade Family
65522	J.W.V.	Schooner	Chester	Point	1871	58	76.0 x 17.9 x 9.6	1903-1909

Notes on History: *Built by John Stephens at Yard Point on Restronguet Creek, South Cornwall (and probably designed by William Ferris), for John William Vinton of Taibach, Glamorganshire, who owned her until 1877. She was then owned in Chester and Connah's Quay until 1892 when she was sold to Watchet and in 1897 to St. Ives. She was run down by a dredger in Southampton Water on March 12th, 1909, when bound for Newport with steel scrap from Southampton. All hands were saved and the vessel was salved and later used as a barge at Par. She was a ketch when owned by the Slades and George Quance.*

Number	Name	Main Port of Registration	Rig	Where built	When built	Tons	Dimensions	Period owned by Slade Family
91320	Maud Mary	Bideford	Ketch	Howden Dyke	1889	62	77.2 × 20.6 × 9.4	1908-1918

Notes on History: *First owned by G. H. Anderton of Howden, Yorkshire, and sold to William Quance, who in turn sold her to Matthew Butcher of Yarmouth. An auxiliary engine of 50 h.p. was fitted when she was bought by William Gibbs of Cardiff in 1923. She came back to Appledore in 1925, and was converted to a three-masted schooner with the same type of rig as the "Haldon" in 1930. She was later owned in Weston-super-Mare, Almouth and Plymouth before she was sold to Polish owners and put under command of Michael Leszczynski. She was lost on the south coast of England in 1939.*

Number	Name	Main Port of Registration	Rig	Where built	When built	Tons	Dimensions	Period owned by Slade Family
58680	St. Agnes	Hayle	Schooner	St. Agnes	1872	58	66.2 x 20.2 x 9.0	1905-1906

Notes on History: *Owned by Martin Hitchins and John Hitchins of St. Agnes, Cornwall, until bought by Thomas Slade. Stranded and became total loss on Inwards Rocks, River Severn, while coal laden for Fremington from Lydney. She was attempting to seek shelter in Chepstow river. All hands were saved.*

Number	Name	Main Port of Registration	Rig	Where built	When built	Tons	Dimensions	Period owned by Slade Family
67966	Elizabeth Jane	Chester	Schooner	Connah's Quay	1875	88	80.3 x 21.6 x 10.5	1910-1916

Notes on History: *Built for Humphrey Foulkes of Connah's Quay and owned there until bought by George Quance and W. K. Slade. Lost with all hands off Cork Harbour 1916.*

Number	Name	Rig	Main Port of Registration	Where built	When built	Tons	Dimensions	Period owned by Slade Family
81756	Doris	Schooner	Salcombe	Salcombe	1880	78	80.0 x 20.4 x 9.9	1910-1918

Notes on History: *First owned by W. W. Steer of Salcombe and then by Edward Hamblin of Bridgwater and W. Morgan Lewis of Cardiff. Converted to ketch rig by Thomas Slade in 1914. Stranded at Isigny, France, 1918, broke her back and sank.*

Number	Name	Rig	Main Port of Registration	Where built	When built	Tons	Dimensions	Period owned by Slade Family
68590	Lady of the Lake	Ketch	Portsmouth	Bosham	1876	84	78.1 x 19.6 x 9.6	1911-1916

Notes on History: *Built for, and probably by, Thomas Smart of Bosham. Thomas Smart managed small fleet of schooners and brigantines which brought coal from N.E. coast to Bosham, they would sometimes take away a cargo of corn. Owned by Smart family until 1910. Bought by Sarah Quance the next year and sunk by a submarine on November 28th, 1916, thirty-five miles south east of the Start on a voyage to Treport with coal from Bristol Channel. The crew were rescued from their own boat by a passing steamer.*

Number	Name	Main Port of Registration	Rig	Where built	When built	Tons	Dimensions	Period owned by Slade Family
86466	Progress	Salcombe	Ketch	Kingsbridge	1884	76	80.2 × 19.2 × 9.2	1912-1946

Notes on History: *Built for North Atlantic trade to Newfoundland in which she ran for nineteen years under command of Captain Shepherd and ownership of Henry Grant of Salcombe. During this time she once sailed from Newfoundland to Bristol Channel in fourteen days and on another occasion carried her mizzen gaff topsail all the way from Cape Race to Gibraltar. She once touched the submerged shelf of an iceberg, but sailed off unhurt. On another occasion she was hove to for thirty days and suffered damage to the bulwarks. Her last Newfoundland voyage was made in 1908. She was bought by Thomas Slade in 1912 and an auxiliary motor of 40 h.p. was fitted in 1918. Used as balloon barrage vessel during Second World War, she was bought by the Harris family and refitted as a ketch in 1950. She was sold and laid up at Milford some years later and at the time this book was written was lying derelict in a creek off Milford Haven. A number of her fittings are now preserved in the National Maritime Museum.*

Number	Name	Main Port of Registration	Rig	Where built	When built	Tons	Dimensions	Period owned by Slade Family
65043	Millom Castle	Barrow	Schooner	Ulverston	1870	78	81.2 × 20.6 × 9.5	1912-1931

Notes on History: *First owned by William Postlethwaite of Millom, Cumberland, who, in 1880, owned twenty-three schooners, and who sold her to W. K. Slade in 1912. An auxiliary engine of 40 h.p. was fitted in 1919. The vessel was extensively damaged in early 1930's and was surrendered by the Slades. In 1933 she was registered as for harbour work only and was at that time at Plymouth. She is still in existence in a creek in Cornwall.*

I*

Number	Name	Main Port of Registration	Rig	Where built	When built	Tons	Dimensions	Period owned by Slade Family
77419	W. D. Potts	Caernarvon	Schooner	Pwllheli	1878	88	83.0 x 22.0 x 10.4	1916-1917

Notes on History: Last vessel built at Pwllheli. Owned by Williams family there until 1908. Then by Robert Robert of Colwyn Bay until 1916.

Number	Name	Main Port of Registration	Rig	Where built	When built	Tons	Dimensions	Period owned by Slade Family
75264	Trio	Guernsey	Schooner	Jersey	1877	73	77.6 × 19.6 × 9.2	1909-1919

Notes on History: First owned by De La Mere family in Jersey and then in Watchet until 1909. She was rerigged by the Slades as a ketch and earned her purchase price in two years. She was bought by Captain Warren of Bridgwater in 1919, an auxiliary engine of 9 h.p. was fitted in 1926. She was lost by stranding in the River Parret in March, 1939.

Number	Name	Main Port of Registration	Rig	Where built	When built	Tons	Dimensions	Period owned by Slade Family
85958	Haldon	Barnstaple	Ketch	Plymouth	1893	77	88.0 × 21.6 × 9.9	1922-1943

Notes on History: First owned in Topsham and then in Scotland and Ireland and then by Hook Shipping Co. of Haverford-west. W. J. Slade converted her to a three-masted schooner and sold her in 1943. About 1948 she was sold to Continental owners and was still afloat in 1955 as a completely converted, fully powered motor ship, with her accommodation in a raised after structure. She was then trading in Icelandic waters.

Number	Name	Main Port of Registration	Rig	Where built	When built	Tons	Dimensions	Period owned by Slade Family
55374	Margaret Hobley	London	Schooner	Pembroke	1868	124	86.6 × 22.2 × 10.8	1922-1948

Notes on History: *Owned first by Thomas Hobley of Caernarvon and later by William Postlethwaite of Millom. Auxiliary engine of 80 h.p. installed in 1921. Sold to William Quance by the Hook Shipping Co. in 1922 for £1200. Not refitted after balloon barrage service in the Second World War.*

Number	Name	Main Port of Registration	Rig	Where built	When built	Tons	Dimensions	Period owned by Slade Family
29343	Daring	Barnstaple	Ketch	Bideford	1863	63	68.0 x 18.0 x 9.0	1921-1927

Notes on History: *Built by Johnson at Bideford-East-the-Water. Owned in Bideford, Barnstaple and the Isle of Wight before being bought by James Slade. No longer registered in 1928.*

Number	Name	Rig	Main Port of Registration	Where built	When built	Tons	Dimensions	Period owned by Slade Family
102465	Donald & Doris	Schooner	Whitehaven	Amlwch	1897	122	96.7×23.1×10.5	1924-1948

Notes on History: *First owned by Robert Johnson of Millom, and later in Dublin. An auxiliary engine of 50 h.p. fitted in 1923. Not refitted after balloon barrage service in the Second World War.*

Number	Name	Rig	Main Port of Registration	Where built	When built	Tons	Dimensions	Period owned by Slade Family
109732	M. A. James	Schooner	Caernarvon	Portmadoc	1900	97	89.6×22.7×10.6	1930-1948

Notes on History: *Built for the North Atlantic trade to Newfoundland the " M. A. James " was typical of the great series of merchant schooners built at Portmadoc between 1890 and 1913, which in many ways represented the finest development of the British schooner. She was owned until 1917 by John Jones of Portmadoc and later by the Plymouth Co-operative Society from 1919 until W. J. Slade bought her in 1930 for £750 but had to spend £1195 to fit her for sea and install an auxiliary engine of 70 h.p. The last vessel to be bought by the Slades, she was not refitted after balloon barrage service in the Second World War and fell to pieces in the river Torridge. A model of her by W.J. Slade is on display in the National Maritime Museum.*

NOTES ON THE RACING OF SCHOONERS AND KETCHES

OUR VESSELS, ESPECIALLY the small ketches, were not so very much larger than the largest of modern ocean racing yachts. Those who sail for pleasure in these modern craft may like to know something of the way we used to race together in heavy commercial vessels, so I have prepared the following notes on this subject.

When I was a schoolboy living at Appledore there was often great excitement among the sailors, caused by the everlasting endeavours of various skippers to get more speed out of the little ketches, and to a lesser extent out of the schooners. There were some very fast ships belonging to the port and it was always considered an Appledore skipper would certainly get everything out of the ship he sailed. The sails were made to fit properly and the sailmaker was kept on his toes all the time, because, if the cut of a sail did not satisfy the owner as well as the skipper, it had to come ashore again to be altered before payment was made.

Among the most outstanding of the fast craft was the *Heather Bell*, built by Westacott at Barnstaple, the *Alpha* (Plate 1) and *Illelia*, built at Sunny Corner, Truro (all three of these vessels were owned by my family and are listed in Appendix 1), and the *Bonito* and *Leader*, iron ketches converted into cargo vessels from North Sea trawlers. There were several others who were very close competitors, chief among these being our *J.W.V.* after she became ketch rigged. This ship was built by the man who built the famous *Rhoda Mary*, one of the fastest of all the vessels.

There were also some fast ships belonging to Braunton on the River Taw and when, during the Christmas holidays, all the fast ships congregated inside the bar to load gravel for ports in the Bristol Channel it meant every skipper was all out to make a fast passage to secure a good turn for discharging. Those bringing up the rear were likely to make a long round trip, and too often did.

Before my time came to take my part as one of the crew, a race took place between the *Leader* and the *Alpha* and all the old skippers were in an argumentative mood as to who would be the winner. So much excitement prevailed that even the local curate of the church, Mr.

Muller, caught the fever. When the day came for the two to sail from Appledore there was a nice whole sail breeze from a south westerly point. The two came down river on the port tack close together. When they were passing the Royal George Quay all the West Appledore sailors were giving vent to their feelings. The ships were hauled close to the wind, the *Leader* having a good position on the weather quarter of the *Alpha* but the *Alpha* just far enough ahead to avoid being blanketed. I was old enough to understand every move and was, therefore, enthusiastic in the cause of the *Alpha*, skippered by my father. Of course, boys in those days were kept in order and not allowed to have anything to say among grown-ups, but even we boys had our favourite, which was generally the ship the father sailed in. There were various opinions among the men as to whether the *Leader* was crawling up on her opponent, or if it was going the other way. Suddenly I became tense. Old Captain Sam Guard, owner of several ketches, a barquentine and a schooner, exclaimed in a loud voice, " The *Alpha* is going two feet to *Leader's* one." This, of course, was an exaggeration, but although there were arguments and disagreement it gave me a great thrill and I was proud to be Billie Slade, Jun.

Then some of the men went up on the hill (behind West Appledore) to form a better idea, but, of course, the difference in such a short period was hardly noticeable and so both ships went over the bar together. Captain Tom Scilly of the *Leader* was a very fine sailor and the *Leader* never had a better man in charge of her. It was certain that if she failed to beat the *Alpha* it would be through no fault of the man who sailed her.

They disappeared around Baggy Point, still very close to each other. The wind was freshening and Captain Scilly set his balloon staysail in an attempt to pass the *Alpha*. Above Bull Point the wind backed more southerly and the *Alpha* was unable to set the square sail, so was slightly at a disadvantage. In the meantime the curate, Mr. Muller, had disappeared, no one noticed his absence. Then a telegram came from Ilfracombe to the effect that both ships were passing, *Alpha* leading by a short distance. The curate had cycled the twenty-six miles from Appledore to see the race and had sent the telegram home. My knowledge of this race is based on the arguments and seamen's talk overheard after it was over. They may have forgotten it very soon, but my memory of it and the thrill I enjoyed still stands out most vividly.

To continue the race. Both ships kept within a short distance of each other until well above the foreland. They went up clear of the sudden hard squalls which always came off the land in this district when the wind was southerly. But now the wind hauled a point or two more westerly. This was exactly what the *Alpha* was waiting for. Up went her square sail, with the yard braced well forward and the tack set down to the cathead. It was the *Alpha's* turn to have the advantage and they made full use of it. Away went the *Alpha* from the *Leader*. She arrived at Avonmouth jetty first in turn for discharging and had beaten her rival by a reasonable margin.

There were many races among the Braunton and Appledore ships during the construction of Avonmouth docks, but the results were always in favour of the first five I have mentioned if they were among the crowd. Sometimes one would win and sometimes the other, but it was always a close finish. If according to my experience I had to give a candid opinion of which ship was the fastest of the bunch I think I would favour the *Heather Bell* as long as she could carry her light clouts, but in a strong wind I would place the *Bonito* very slightly as favourite, with *Alpha* and *Ulelia* a good match for her in all circumstances. The gravel trade soon finished and races in this direction became very rare. My memory now goes to a race between *J.W.V.* sailed by Captain Philip Quance and the *Ulelia* under my father. Both being bound from Lydney to Castletownshend, a small port between Galley Head and Cape Clear. The *Ulelia* had got down channel ahead of *J.W.V.*, but in bad weather at Christmastime Bideford Bar is a trap and the *Ulelia* went into it about a fortnight before the festive season. Captain Philip Quance stayed on the Penarth mud and he was sensible, for after a day or two, out came the wind north west and down came *J.W.V.* The wind backed south west and Father knew his rival had passed him down on the Saturday night. Now it was a rare occurrence to see Father leave home on a Sunday, but this time he not only wanted to catch the only berth in Castletownshend, but also time was short for getting back home for Christmas. So away we came, Father being determined to overhaul the *J.W.V.* The wind gradually freshened and we were laying our course for the Old Head comfortably on the port tack carrying every stitch of canvas, including balloon staysail. The night passed with little or no rest for any of us and wind still freshening until the *Ulelia's* main rails were very little above water. She was certainly going all out and being driven mercilessly. It simply couldn't last long.

The second evening out the balloon staysail blew to ribbons and didn't need much handling. The working staysail was set and soon after we sighted the Old Head of Kinsale under the lee. The wind went a little more southerly and we hauled down close to the wind, putting in single reefs and taking in the gaff topsail. It was now getting pretty wild and the *Ulelia* was certainly taking some water on board. We made up our minds that *J.W.V.* would have gone windbound so our skipper kept on, quite satisfied he had made up for lost time. We entered Castletownshend the next morning at dawn, but a shock awaited our skipper, he had underestimated his adversary, there she lay in the only berth and had kept her place ahead, berthing the previous night in the dark.

Well, Father was beaten, but all was not lost, away we went ashore to study the position. We sounded the berth on the side of the Quay and he soon discovered there was room for both ships to work if the *J.W.V.* was swung round with her bow the other way. But the consignee of the cargo objected and gave orders to the master of the *J.W.V.* to remain, as, if the *Ulelia* got in, he would have to sell his coal in competition with another merchant. Father laughed and said nothing in reply. When the men went to their dinner our crew swung

the *J.W.V.* round and alongside of the side of the Quay went the *Ulelia*
to begin discharging. Of course this sent the consignee of the *J.W.V.*
in a temper. Then, very quietly, Father said, " You know, Mr.
Hennessey, I would just as soon get £1 out of *J.W.V.* as the *Ulelia.*"
He took in the sentence in silence, then he said " Do you own the
J.W.V., too?" and said Father, " Yes." Well, Mr. H. accepted the
position with a good grace. There was nothing else to do.

We finished discharging together and now the race home started.
Well ballasted we sailed one evening with light easterly winds. We
remained close hauled and within a quarter mile of each other for four
days and nights, both skippers watching each move and ready to take
every advantage. There was little or nothing to chose between them.
Then one night after dark we tacked ship and went towards the Welsh
coast. Father thought the wind was going to favour us. We lost sight
of *J.W.V.* for the first time, she kept her course on the port tack. Father
was wrong for once. The wind went more southerly, the *J.W.V.* got
home at high water winning the race by about one hour. We had to
anchor in Appledore pool through the ebb tide. So we both got back
for Christmas, this time second, but happy because we were home again.

I have so far given accounts of races between ketches, now I will
turn my attention to a schooner race that completely wore me out, as
mate with my father, although I was young enough to stand any
hardship. We had made a voyage to Runcorn from the clay ports in
company with several schooners, ours being the one hundred and
seventy ton schooner *Elizabeth Jane.* Owing to fine weather and a very
dirty bottom we were well and truly beaten, and, of course, Father
had to stand a lot of leg pull from his skipper friends in Marwood's
office. It appears the *Elizabeth Jane* was known as a fairly fast schooner
before we bought her. Now, it was suggested, she had lost her reputation.
Captain Langmaid of the *Susanna* had certainly beaten us and he, at
the present moment, certainly had the laugh over us.

When we sailed from Runcorn our vessel was put on the ground at
Newferry to clean her bottom. We worked all night doing one side
by anchor lamp light. The next day we did the other bottom and on
the high water shifted off to our anchorage ready for sea. In due course
we left with the rest of the fleet to meet adverse winds fairly strong.

We beat down St. George's channel having plenty of hard work and
hardly any sleep as far as I was concerned. We finally got across to
Trevose with the *Susanna*, all the others having gone windbound. Now
came the test. We were both under small sail blowing very hard from
a south south west point. The *Susanna* was on our weather quarter.
The order came, " Set the boom jib ! Shake a reef out of the mainsail !
Give her the topgallant sail ! " It was done and away we marched from
Susanna. All night she was driven to the limit down on port tack. The
next morning there was no sign of the *Susanna*, the wind veered westerly
and we fetched round the Longships on the starboard tack. We
completed our journey, discharged on a Cornish beach, working day
and night, proceeded into Falmouth harbour where we found *Susanna*
with her cargo still in her, not started to discharge. We had certainly

vindicated the reputation of the *Elizabeth Jane* and Captain Langmaid was the first to congratulate our skipper on his fine performance. In August, 1910, we arrived to Lydney on the early morning tide in company with the ketch *Maud Mary* (Plate 8) owned by my uncle. Our ship, the *Elizabeth Jane*, and *Maud Mary* both loaded coal for Ballinacurra in Cork Harbour, sailing the next tide. *Maud Mary* was a fairly good ship and although not classed with the fastest she was capable of holding her own amongst most sailing coasters. We knew she was a good match for the *Elizabeth Jane* and anticipated a good show. We proceeded as usual getting to Penarth the first ebb where we anchored to await the next ebb tide. Leaving on the next high water, it was soon obvious, in working short tacks on the first of the ebb along the shore, that the *Maud Mary* would get ahead of us. When the full ebb tide made away and we could make longer tacks, we could hold our own quite well. We both got some distance below the Scarweather and not far apart when the wind came off the land. Before long the *Elizabeth Jane* drew slightly ahead. The wind drew more north east as we proceeded, very fine, and were able to set our squaresail, while *Maud Mary* set her balloon staysail, rigged out with the boom kept for this purpose. We passed to southward of the Smalls in the afternoon with wind freshening to a comfortable breeze. All the following night we kept fairly close together, but the next morning we were about one mile ahead and, rounding Rochespoint, anchored together within fifteen minutes. We had done approximately two hundred miles and only about fifteen minutes difference in our speed.

We discharged our cargoes and both loaded oats for Southampton. In about a week we left together with a fine breeze north west. Twenty-four hours later we were going up across Mounts Bay and were so close together that I could read the *Maud Mary's* name on her port bow. We set two light three cornered sails above our topgallant yard, but, although we kept ahead, the difference in speed was almost nothing. As we proceeded up channel the wind freshened from a south south west point and became very dirty. We picked up the Needles and right to the end of this journey both ships kept within a mile of each other, the *Elizabeth Jane* still slightly leading.

We discharged our oats, *Maud Mary* loaded loom at Hamble for Newport (Monmouthshire) and the *Elizabeth Jane* loaded railway chairs at Redbridge for Newport. Both left their respective berths at the same time and met in " Jack in the Basket " which is a recognised anchorage inside the Isle of Wight and opposite Yarmouth. The next high water we sailed with a westerly wind and it was *Maud Mary's* turn to lead. For several days in fine weather we in *Elizabeth Jane* did all we could to keep with her. We succeeded to such an extent that we rounded the Longships together within hailing distance. Then we had the wind astern light and *Elizabeth Jane* drew slightly ahead about a quarter of a mile. We were both short of bread and on losing the wind altogether off St. Ives the *Maud Mary* put out her boat, came up alongside and the boat was manned by part of each ship's crew, including me. It was quite a distance to pull ashore but it was done with very little trouble because the crew were all Appledore men born and brought up in boats. We returned just as the breeze was freshening again from a westerly direction. The *Elizabeth Jane's* yards were kept braced up until the *Maud Mary* came alongside. Her boat was hoisted and away we went again. A day or two after we arrived to Newport with *Elizabeth Jane* still finishing with a slight lead. We had travelled a distance of approximately eight hundred and fifty miles together with a distance between us of never more than one mile.

I will close these short narratives on races by giving my experience of a short race from Holyhead to Fishguard, in which some of the reputed fastest schooners took part. I, myself, was master in the ketch *Trio*, built at Jersey, Channel Islands. The *Millom Castle* and the *Isabella* (both " Barrow flats "), the *Rhoda Mary* and *Katie Cluett* (celebrated flyers, see " The Merchant Schooners," Vol. 2, Chapter 4) and my own little *Trio*, not considered very fast, but very weatherly in heavy weather, were all in it. During the dark hours after leaving we had lost sight of all but the *Katie Cluett* and on the second evening we were below Bardsey Island on the starboard tack blowing strong south west and coming dark. It was in the month of November, as far as my memory goes, 1917.

We saw the *Katie Cluett*, who was only a few hundred yards on our weather, start to reef, and I decided to reef the *Trio*. We took her gaff topsail in, put two rolls in the mainsail and hauled down a single reef in the mizzen (points reefing). In the darkness we lost the *Katie Cluett* and I decided to go all out for Fishguard. We were at this time about halfway down Cardigan Bay with tide turning in our favour. I kept going on starboard tack until I was well in the Bay, then tacked and we picked up the light on Fishguard Pier some distance on the port bow. We were now in smooth water and at 9 p.m. I anchored at Fishguard. At 11 p.m. the *Katie Cluett* came in, the *Rhoda Mary* in the early hours, but she had been down further and run back while the *Katie Cluett* had come straight in without going down further. The *Millom Castle* came in about 9 o'clock the next morning and the *Isabella* later in the day. Both the latter ships had not attempted to go any further than Fishguard. I am not suggesting the *Trio* was a faster ship than the others, perhaps we gained by going in the Bay and down in smooth water. I do not know how we managed to beat the others, it was the first time I had ever been in company with the great racers of Cornish builders and I had beaten them both. Bearing these facts in mind I have often wondered if these crack racers were really all they were supposed to be. A lot depended on those who sailed them. The *Rhoda Mary* and the *Katie Cluett* were undoubtedly very fast, but I still believe there were others equally fast.

W. J. SLADE

APPENDIX 3

NOTE BY CAPTAIN J. WHITEFIELD, D.S.C., EXTRA MASTER'S CERTIFICATE, WHICH AUTHENTICATES W. J. SLADE'S NARRATIVE

CAPTAIN W. J. SLADE and I have been friends for many years and I have been very interested in the book he has written concerning the life of the men and boys who made up the crews of the large number of schooners and ketches owned at Appledore and sailing out of that port. For many years the smaller of these ships, mostly ketches, loaded gravel for Avonmouth and after discharging there proceeded to Lydney to load coal back to Bideford, Appledore and Barnstaple.

The larger vessels traded mostly from Lydney to the small ports in the South of Ireland and usually back to the Bristol Channel or the English Channel ports with oats, timber, etc., and then with china clay to Runcorn and at times to the Thames and to the near Continental ports.

Quite a number of the Appledore ships were owned and sailed by members of one family. Captain Slade's family, for instance, owned quite a number of ships, and when at the age of twelve he went to sea it was in one of the Slade family ships of which his father was master and part owner.

He started as "boy" and gradually got promoted to O.S., A.B., mate and master, and after a time he became part owner, and he put in the whole of his seagoing life in these vessels. I do not know of anyone who knows more about life in these ships than Captain Slade, or more about the upkeep, chartering, insurance, etc., of this type of vessel.

Now my life, starting in the same way, took a different course from Captain Slade's. I was born at Clovelly and my father owned and sailed the three-masted schooner *Polly and Emily*, three hundred tons deadweight and when I was fourteen years of age I left school and joined the *Polly and Emily* in London and my father discharged an A.B. and signed me on as boy, but, of course, I had to do the work of an A.B. and did not get any wages. I expect that I knew as much then as many A.B.s, as every summer I went to sea during our holidays and had to work as one of the crew, so I was not a greenhorn. When I was sixteen years of age I was put mate and was left to carry out all a mate's duties. Up to the age of eighteen I had had no wages and had to be content with two shillings or two shillings and sixpence passed over to me about every four or five weeks, so I thought it time I got some wages. After several hours argument I accepted two pounds ten shillings per month, the proper wages of a mate was four pounds per month.

When twenty years of age I decided to make a break and told my father that I was leaving and going into steam. I did not see any point in going in sail as on a number of occasions I was called up in my watch below to go up and furl sails when A.B.s who had been deepwater refused to go aloft and furl them as they thought the sails should have been taken in before. My father was not a cruel man but was a hard driver and we very rarely went in windbound as the *Polly and Emily* would stand up to any weather. I feel that with over six years experience on the coast I can bear out that what Captain Slade has written about life on the coast in the small vessels is correct, it was a hard life, but I think it made men of those who could stick it and I know in after years my experience on the coast stood me in good stead and gave me confidence to take my ship anywhere.

It seems rather interesting to me how great a difference there was in my early days between Appledore and Clovelly. Clovelly was a small village with a population of only about four hundred people, but almost every man there was a seaman, but nearly all deepwater men, and at one time one could count at least thirty-four Clovelly men who had their master's certificates and they were masters in squareriggers, liners and tramps. Only two coasters were owned in Clovelly, viz., *The Rival*, a small schooner owned and sailed by Captain I. Jones and the other the *Polly and Emily*, owned and sailed by my father, John Whitefield. At Appledore there were over a hundred schooners and ketches owned and sailing out of that port, and after spells of bad weather it was nothing unusual to see sixty to seventy of them going out over the bar on one tide. At Appledore there were few deepwater men, as there were so many small vessels that were trading home most of the time.